You Can Weave!

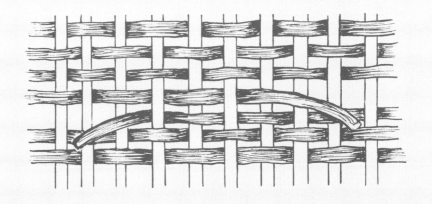

Namak donneh, or salt bag, from India. Many different weaving techniques are combined on the saddle bags and salt bags from this region. The unique shape of this bag is designed to keep the salt, stored in the lower compartment, dry and safe from spilling. The central panels feature flat, slit-woven tapestry surrounded by supplemental weft techniques. Only one side of the bag is ornate, the back is woven in a simple stripe pattern and would be the side facing the wall or next to the animal. Cotton warp, wool weft. From the collection of Jane Schelly.

You Can Weave!

PROJECTS FOR YOUNG WEAVERS

Kathleen Monaghan
Hermon Joyner

Davis Publications, Inc.
Worcester, Massachusetts

ISBN: 087192-493-5

10 9 8 7 6 5 4 3 2 1

Publisher: Wyatt Wade
Editorial Director: Claire Mowbray Golding
Production Editors: Laura Marshall Alavosus, Nancy Burnett
Manufacturing Coordinator: Georgiana Rock
Design: Janis Owens
Photographs: Hermon Joyner
Front Cover: *Background:* Kumihimo braids by Jean Parodi. *Clockwise from right:* Polish tapestry wallhanging, collection of Ruth Beal; Mexican fringe, collection of Sue Ellen Heflin; students at work.
Back Cover: *Clockwise from top:* Guatemalan headband; students at work; Canadian Fabric, collection of Ruth Beal.

Printed in China

Contents

Bright flowers are embroidered on this detail of a warp-faced shirt from Mexico. The warp threads are packed closely together, making the weft thread almost invisible. Cotton and metallic warp and embroidery threads, cotton weft. From the collection of Sue Ellen Heflin.

Acknowledgements

I wish to thank my colleagues and classmates in the Lesley College Creative Arts in Learning Group III. The wonderful diversity and enthusiasm of these educators has surprised and inspired me. The process of learning with, and from, them has been tremendous fun. Special thanks to Nancy Ingerson and Denise Briggs for field testing these lessons with their sixth grade classes and giving me valuable feedback.

I appreciate the generosity of my friends, fellow teachers, and members of the Spokane Handweaver's Guild who loaned me items from their textile collections. Jane Schelly, Lars Neises, and Ruth Beal were so very helpful in giving me access to their beautiful weaving collections.

Thank you to my wonderful students who helped me develop these lessons, loaned me their projects, and modeled for pictures. My patient models were Kennedy Kearney-Fisher, Margeaux Fox, David A. Brady, Nevin Banicki, Greg Shintani, Anik Karim, Kyle Percy, Clair Monaghan, Annie Iverson, Hannah and Gray Lindberg.

Student artwork was supplied by Hannah Lindberg, Angie Lloyd, Janessa Cocchiarella, Amy M. Marsh, Orion Buske, Peter Zysk, Leah G. Jordan, Courtney Rowland, Whitney Porter, James Clark, Jesse Lee Ashby, Vitaliy Grishko, Shyelle Dyck, Kimberly Janssen, Jennie Morefield, Lindsey A. Ridgway, Caitlin Keogh, Sara Shelton, Elizabeth M. Matresse, David Aberasturi, Heather Bowman, Annie Johnston, and Megan Galvan.

Thanks also to my daughter who has endured being ignored while I worked at the computer. And especially to my husband who supported me in many ways, photographing, proofing, critiquing, and suggesting new approaches.

Preface

As an elementary art specialist working in the public schools, I have the opportunity to teach a wide variety of students. We work with drawing and painting materials, papier-mâché, and clay. I have been impressed with the skill, talent, and enthusiasm of my students, and enchanted with the beauty of their artwork.

As a fiber artist, I have high expectations of how weaving should look. Initially, I thought that my students were too young to tackle the process of weaving. But, research into other cultures proved this assumption to be wrong. In cultures around the world, where weaving is still central to the day-to-day life of families, children learn to weave proficiently by the age of seven or eight. If those children can do it, why not my students?

As I examined this question, I realized how often students use art materials in their other classes. Classroom teachers in the elementary levels introduce students to many basic skills which art teachers build upon. Most of my fourth grade students have used some sort of clay, have painted with watercolors, drawn with pencils, and colored with crayons. They have come to understand the subtle differences of the materials. They know that by pressing harder on the crayon, the color gets darker. Not many, however, have learned the fundamentals or vocabulary of weaving.

To get the weaving results I wanted in the classroom, I needed a sequence of lessons that would build a basic level of knowledge and skill and progress by small steps. The lessons in this book are set up to allow teachers to introduce the basic elements of weaving to their students without having to be experts themselves. By working through the lessons, you will build the vocabulary necessary for understanding the process and the skills necessary to produce good work. Specialists who see students from many grades for more than one year may want to divide the lessons into grade levels to build on each year's experience.

Because funds for equipment and supplies often are limited, all the lessons rely on supplies that are readily available in most schools. Students can easily build many of the looms. The lessons mirror the technological advances in weaving which have occurred in cultures throughout the world. The beginning projects use few tools but rely on laborious counting of "over and under." Each project introduces a technological advance and a new challenge. By the time they are weaving on a backstrap loom, students will have experienced tremendous change in the basic process of weaving.

As you prepare to work with your class, read through the lesson, assemble the materials, and then read the lesson again with the materials in front of you. It may be helpful to do the project yourself before presenting it to students. It is important to work through the sections in order, as the later projects assume knowledge and skills from earlier projects. The last four lessons, however, can be done at anytime.

I hope you and your students have a wonderful experience with these lessons. Although I originally designed the projects to be used with young students, they are fun for any age, and the sequence will make sense to anyone who wants to learn to weave.

Kathleen Monaghan

In the region from India to the Mediterranean Sea, there is a tradition of flat woven rugs, called kilims. Kilims feature bold geometric design, multiple borders, and often use slit tapestry joining techniques. These small slits give a crisp edge to the shapes, since the colors do not share a common warp. Cotton warp and weft. From the collection of Jane Schelly.

CHAPTER 1

The Weaving Process

Weaving uses two sets of thread or yarn — the warp and the weft — to make cloth. The **warp** threads are held under tension, usually on a loom. The loom may be as simple as a piece of cardboard with yarn wound around it. The **weft,** or woof as it once was called, crosses the warp threads at a right angle. In order to create a strong fabric, the weft weaves over and under the warp threads. Because the warp threads are under tension and will be subjected to some friction during weaving, these threads need to be strong and smooth. The weft may be exactly the same material as the warp or some other type of yarn or thread.

The following projects introduce students to the basic terms and techniques of the weaving process.

A group of sisters sat, spinning and weaving

together, happy in their daily chores.

One sister said, as she thumbed her thread

into a fine strand, "Let others run away

from housework, Minerva is our goddess,

ruler of these crafts and their attendant wisdom,

better than most gods I've ever known.

Come, let us enjoy these hours together

and tell stories as we work, each of us

listening closely to one another."

The Metamorphoses,
Ovid

Woven Paper Place Mat

Paper weaving is a fast and inexpensive way to introduce students to the weaving process. The following lesson builds on the basic over-and-under technique of weaving. Once students understand this concept, they can experiment with different color and weave combinations.

Vocabulary

warp, weft, weave, plain weave, basket weave, twill

Materials

Each student will need:
Construction paper: 9 x 12" (23 x 30 cm) and 1 x 9" (3 x 23 cm) strips, various colors
Pencil
Scissors
Glue
Ruler

Paper is a familiar material to students of any age. Paper weaving allows students to quickly learn basic techniques and try new ideas with confidence.

The finished woven paper can be used for place mats, book covers, or other decorative purposes.

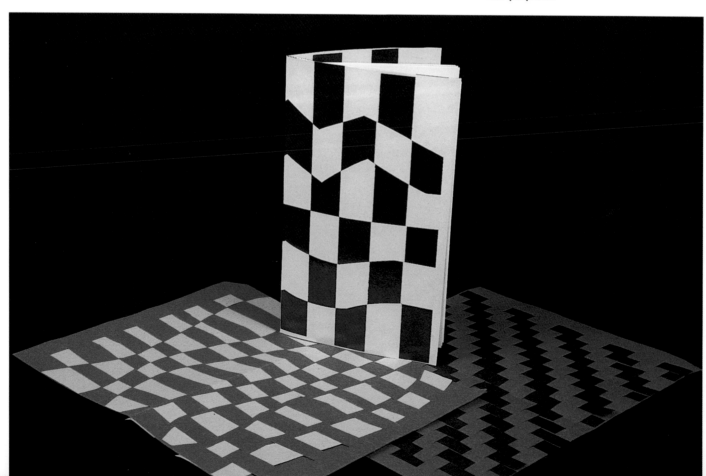

Plain Weave

The **plain weave** pattern is the simplest weave structure. Demonstrate the following steps for students, then circulate among them and help as necessary.

1 Choose one sheet of paper. This will be the warp. Fold the paper in half (to measure 9 x 6"; 23 x 15 cm) and draw a line approximately 1" (3 cm) from the open end. This line will be a guideline for cutting.

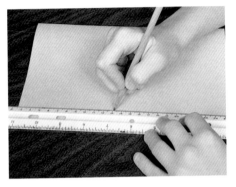

Make sure students draw their guidelines at the open end of the paper, not at the center fold.

2 Now draw 5-6 lines from the fold to the guideline. The lines may be straight or curved. Make sure the lines are not too close to the edge of the paper. Curved lines should not be too complex or the project will be difficult to weave.

Five or six lines will give the first-time weaver enough of a design in the finished project without being too difficult.

3 With the paper still folded, cut along the lines from the fold to the guideline. Unfold the paper. These strips are the warps.

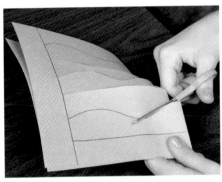

If lines are gently curved, they will be easier to cut, and will weave without catching on the weft strips.

4 Using a different color strip of 1 x 9" (3 x 23 cm) paper, begin weaving across the warp in an over-one, under-one pattern. If the weft begins over the warp in the first row, begin the next row under the warp. It is the alternating rows that create a solid structure in weaving. Continue weaving this pattern until all the warps are full. Make sure that there is no extra room between weft rows. The pattern is much more striking and successful if the wefts are packed tightly together.

Students will be motivated if they can see the pattern clearly as they weave. Have them watch the pattern emerge as they start at the bottom of the paper and pack each weft strip firmly next to the row below.

5 Glue the edges down on both sides of the paper.

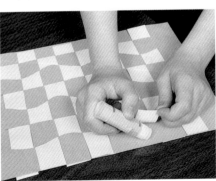

Gluing the ends down will make students' weavings more secure.

By combining thin and thick warps and wefts, students can achieve very interesting and complex patterns.

Variations

Encourage students to try some interesting variations using plain weave. Demonstrate the following.

- Vary the shape and size of the warps. Try combinations of thick and thin warps. Repeat the thick and thin pattern in the weft.

- Vary the size and color of the wefts. Try to create a pattern in the color of the wefts.

- Try cutting shaped wefts. It is very important to weave in each weft before cutting the next. The wefts must be woven in the same order as they are cut for the shapes to interlock.

- Use patterned or printed papers for warp or weft. Try weaving two images together. Consider the content of the image and weave similar or opposite ideas (i.e., pictures of different plants for similar content or images of night and day for opposites).

- Using a third sheet of paper, cut out an interesting shape from the middle of the sheet and glue the remainder of the paper over the finished weaving. The positive shape in the middle will be the weaving showing through.

- Use a small stamp to print a pattern on the warp or weft.

- Choose a color picture from a magazine and photocopy it. Cut one copy for warp and one for weft. Weave the two images together, matching areas as carefully as possible.

- Draw or paint on the warp paper. This can be done before or after cutting the warps.

- Use the finished paper weavings as cards or covers of journals and photo albums.

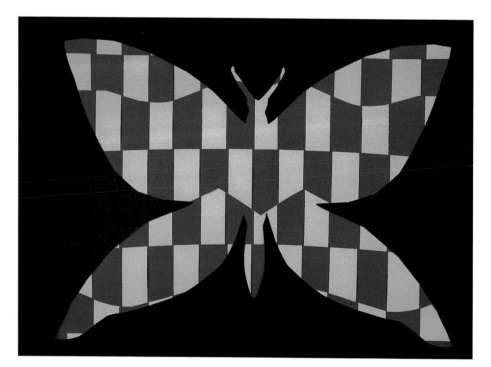

Cutting out a simple, bold shape and gluing it over the woven paper makes a dramatic design.

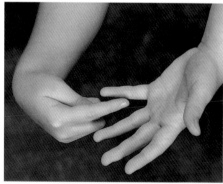

Have students practice making a plain-weave pattern by weaving one index finger through the fingers on their other hand. Explain that the fingers of one hand are like the warp, and the index finger moving between them is like the weft.

Basket Weave

Basket weave is very similar to plain weave. Instead of the over-one, under-one pattern of plain weave, basket weave uses an over-two, under-two pattern. This gives a wider spacing to the warps. Use a wider strip of weft to balance the wider warp.

Learning basket weave is an intermediate step for learning twill — a more complicated weaving technique that allows a great variety of patterns.

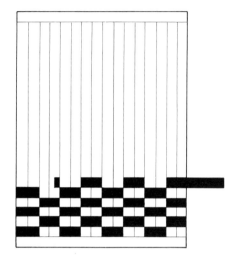

Twill

The fabric of a pair of jeans is an example of twill. **Twill** is a pattern of over-two, under-two that stair-steps over one warp on each row. This forms the diagonal line in denim. To demonstrate a straight twill pattern for students, begin as before with a folded 9 x 12" (23 x 30 cm) paper, but cut 15 straight lines every ½" (1 cm). This produces 16 warps. Unfold the paper and number the warps, left to right, from 1 to 4, repeating 3 times.

Weave as follows:

Row one: weave under all warps numbered 1 and 2 (repeat to end of row)

Row two: weave under all warps numbered 2 and 3 (repeat to end of row)

Row three: weave under all warps numbered 3 and 4 (repeat to end of row)

Row four: weave under all warps numbered 4 and 1 (repeat to end of row)

Repeat rows 1–4 to the end of paper.

Variations

Once students have mastered a straight twill, have them experiment with some of these variations, or invite them to make up their own.

• Begin weaving as above but, after row 4, do not go back to row 1. Instead, reverse the order and weave row 3, then 2, then 1. Continue weaving rows 1, 2, 3, 4, 3, 2, 1, 2, 3, 4, and so on to create a zigzag pattern called a **vertical point twill**.

• Try a different sequence of numbers at the top of the page. Labeling the warps 1, 2, 3, 4, 3, 2, and so on, and weaving in any of the patterns above will create interesting zigzags and diamonds.

• Try alternating colors or size of weft. Keep in mind, however, that too many different colors or sizes in one piece will overpower the weave structure.

• Use a magazine picture or text as the warp or weft. Try different combinations of plain paper, text, and photographs.

• Combine rows of plain weave with twill.

Foreign newspapers can be an interesting source of weaving material.

Students can make two images gradually blend together by weaving them into each other.

Straw Weaving

This straw weaving lesson gives students a chance to weave with yarn and practice the over/under technique. In straw weaving, the weft threads are packed closely together, completely covering the warps. This creates a weft-faced fabric. Straw weaving helps students gain the skills and confidence needed for more advanced weaving projects.

Vocabulary

warp, weft, weave, weft-faced

Materials

Each student will need:

Straws: 5 beverage straws cut in
   half
Yarn for warp: 5 pieces, 12–14"
   (31–36 cm) long, worsted weight
   rug yarn
Masking tape: 5 pieces, 1" (3 cm)
   long
Yarn for weft: 8 yards total, several
   different colors
Wire loop (optional)

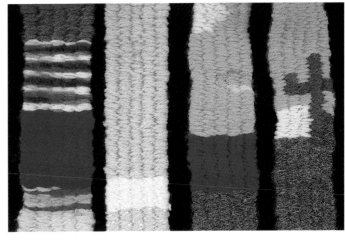

The straw-woven belt on the left is by a fourth grade student. The belt on the right is by a sixth grade teacher who incorporated tapestry techniques with straw weaving.

This narrow headband from Guatemala is a great example of a weft-faced fabric. Cotton, approximately ½ x 45" (1 x 114 cm).

Setting Up the Straw Loom

Follow these steps to make looms for very young students. Demonstrate the process for older students.

1 Thread five warp yarns through the straws. You can use a wire with a small loop on the end to pull the thread through the straw.

2 Use a small piece of tape on the end of each straw to secure ½" (1 cm) of yarn to the outside of the straw.

3 Knot all the warps together at the opposite end.

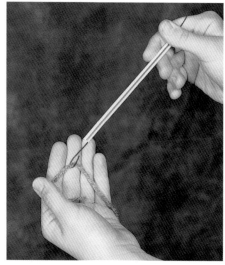

A threading hook, made from any thin wire, will make it easy to thread the warp through each straw. Always provide adult supervision when students use this tool.

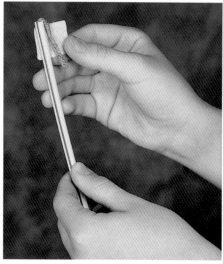

Have students tape the ends of their straws as neatly as possible. If the tape is rough, it will continually catch the weft yarn and slow down students' weaving.

Weaving a Bookmark

Explain the following steps as you demonstrate them for students.

1 Hold all the straws in one hand between your palm and your thumb.

Remind students to hold the straws firmly as they begin to weave. After they have several rows woven, the straws will stay in place by themselves.

2 With your other hand, weave a one-yard length of weft around each of the straws. You can anchor the weft with the thumb holding the straws in place. Start at one side and weave to the other. Come around the last straw and weave back to where you began. Continue weaving in this manner until you reach the end of the first weft.

3 Tie your second weft thread onto the end of the first and continue weaving. As the weaving progresses, you will no longer need to hold the straws in place; the weft will do that. As you weave, gently slide the weft down an inch at a time. Eventually the weft will fill all the straws and "fall off" the end onto the warp thread. This is good because you want to have all the weft off the straws at the end of the project. However, if you slide all the weft off the straws before you are

finished weaving, the straws will no longer be in order and it will be hard to continue the weaving.

Students should let the weft build up on the straws, then push it down an inch at a time.

Once students have completely filled the straws with weft, they can let some of the weaving fall off the straws onto the warp threads. Point out that the first few rows of weaving will loosen up after they are off the straws, but they will be packed firmly again as the weaving progresses.

4 Continue to add weft in the color sequence of your choice, and ease the weaving down the straws and the warp.

When students wish to change colors, or run out of weft thread, have them simply tie a new color onto the old one and keep weaving.

5 When the weaving is as long as desired, pull the tape off the straws. Slide the warps out of the straws and tie a knot close to the last weft. Once both ends are knotted, you can slide the weft around on the warp threads to make the weaving more even.

The weaving will bunch up somewhat as students remove the straws. This will even out once all the straws are removed.

Variations

• To simplify this project, have students use only one color of yarn. Do not cut the yarn into lengths before starting. Provide balls of yarn and instruct students to just pick up the end and leave the yarn attached to the ball. Variegated yarn will produce stripes in the weave without students having to change threads.

• If students choose to make a belt or guitar strap, have them start with warp threads 12" (30 cm) longer than the desired finished length.

Webster's defines a group of geese as a flock, but a flock of geese in flight is called a skein.

If you are working from skeins of yarn, rather than balls, have students work in pairs to wind the yarn into balls. Make sure that you find the center of the loop before you cut off any ties that are holding it together. If you are working from pull-skeins, be sure to start the skein from the thread on the inside of the skein, not the outside. This will prevent the yarn from rolling around the floor.

Movement

Physical action can help students visualize and understand weaving patterns. To present the over one, under one pattern, have a group of 6–8 student volunteers be the warps. Ask them how a warp would stand. Would it be crumpled up? All tangled together? Remind them that warps hold still. Have them line up, with enough space between them for a person to pass. Then, have another student act as the weft, passing between each warp. As the weft passes behind or in front of each warp end, ask the class to say "over" or "under." When the weft reaches the end of the row, have the student return in the opposite over/under pattern.

Writing

Have students choose two opposite concepts (bad/good, earth/sky, past/future) and find or create images that convey those ideas. Ask them to cut one picture for warps, one for wefts, and weave them together in a pattern of their choice. Then, have students write a diamonte poem to match the two words.

Art History

Show students the work of M. C. Escher. Then, have students choose images as above, but rather than cut and weave the entire picture, have them weave together the edges of the pictures. The weaving will appear to change from one image to the other.

Math

Students can design various weaves by using colored pencils and standard graph paper. Each horizontal row represents a weft thread, each vertical row represents a warp thread. Begin with two colored pencils, one color for warp and a different color for weft. If the weft is on top of the warp, color that square the weft color. If the weft is under the warp, color that square the warp color. If the pattern is over-two, under-two, then two squares next to each other will be the same color. Continue for each row until the pattern emerges.

When designing their own weaves on graph paper, limit students to no more than three squares of one color in a horizontal or vertical row. In real weaving, skipping over large numbers of threads at one time creates an unstable weave. Suggest that students try this with paper weaving to see what happens.

Even young students do very well with straw weaving. They can make small projects, such as bookmarks, or larger projects, such as belts and scarves.

CHAPTER 2

Cardboard Looms

Once students are comfortable with the basics of warp, weft, and plain weave, and have practiced them with paper and straw weaving, they are ready to use a simple loom. One of the easiest and most versatile looms begins with a piece of cardboard. Students can create simple ribbon weaving, pouches, and more complex tapestry pictures on various weights of cardboard.

Arachnids, or spiders, are named for the Greek weaver, Arachne, who challenged the goddess Athene to a weaving contest. Her skill angered Athene, who tore up Arachne's tapestry. Poor Arachne hung herself and was then changed into a spider.

The New Book of Goddesses and Heroines
Patricia Monaghan

A highly skilled tapestry artist will use many different values of a color to give the picture a sense of depth. The artist begins with a very detailed drawing of the scene, fully shaded, which hangs behind her warp threads as the tapestry is woven. *Orange Blossom Special*, 1996 by Sarah Swett. Handspun wool and mohair, natural dyes, 46 x 60" (117 x 152 cm). Photo by Mark LaMoreaux.

Ribbon Weaving

This project introduces students to using a cardboard loom with string warp. The weft strips in this project are cut the same width as the cardboard, and are not woven back and forth across the warp. This allows students to become comfortable with warping and weaving before they attempt more challenging techniques.

Vocabulary
weft-faced

Materials
Each student will need:

Cardboard: about 8 x 10" (20 x 25 cm). Recycled cereal boxes work well.

Scissors

Ruler

Pencil

Masking tape: 2 pieces, 1" (3 cm) long

String for warp: thin, strong, and smooth; about 8 yards for each project

Ribbon, yarn, or paper for weft: strips of different widths cut into lengths to match the width of the cardboard

Ribbon weavings are a great introduction to weaving on a cardboard loom. They can include a wide range of weft colors and textures.

⌗ Making the Loom

Have students create their looms as you demonstrate the following steps.

1 Mark every ¼" (½ cm) along the two short sides of the cardboard. With scissors, cut a small line on each mark, about ½" (1 cm) long. These cuts are the notches that will hold the warp threads.

Have students start and end the warping by taping the thread to the back of the cardboard. The warp will be wound onto the front of the board.

2 Tape the yarn to one side of the cardboard. This will be the back of the loom. Pass the thread through the first notch to the opposite end of the loom. Wrap the thread through this notch to the back, through the second notch to the front, and back to where you began.

Show students how to take the warp through one notch, around the back, and forward through the next notch. If warp threads are too tight, the cardboard loom will bend and curl. Monitor students' work, helping individuals as necessary.

3 Pass the thread through this second notch, to the back. Come around notch number 2, through number 3 from behind, and along the front to notches 3 and 4 on the other end.

4 Continue winding the warp thread this way until all the notches are full. The warp should be only on one side of the cardboard. If it is on both sides, then the threads are not being brought around the notches, only through them.

5 Tape the end of the thread to the back.

⌗ Weaving

Refer back to the paper weaving project and review the plain weave pattern with students. Tell them they can weave the same pattern on their cardboard looms. Remind them to begin at one end with a weft strip, weaving over one, under one, across the warp threads, then to continue with the next row, making sure to alternate with the row below. Have students repeat this pattern until no more wefts can fit onto the cardboard. Explain that, because the warp is thinner than the weft, more of the weft will be visible. This is called a **weft-faced** weave.

Remind students to check the pattern of each row as they weave.

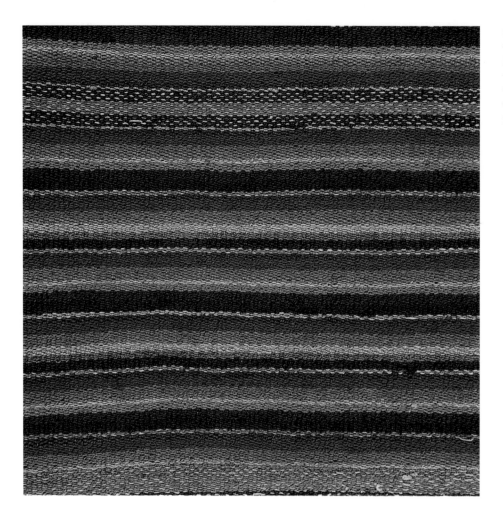

Narrow horizontal stripes blend together when the colors are similar to each other. Notice how the reds and browns blend from light to dark in this detail of a weft-faced, plain weave fabric from India. Wool warp and weft, from the collection of Jane Schelly.

Finishing

The weaving may be removed from the cardboard or left attached. If the cardboard is removed, students may want to add a small dowel at the top of their weavings. Students also may wish to add beads, charms, or other small ornaments to the end of their weavings.

Woven Pouch

Vocabulary
weft-faced

Materials
Each student will need:

Cardboard: about 3 x 8" (8 x 20 cm). The cardboard must be thin enough to bend in half, but stiff enough to hold the warps tight. Recycled cereal boxes work well.

Tapestry needle: large-eyed

Scissors

Ruler

Pencil or pen

Plastic or metal fork

String for warp: thin, strong, and smooth; about 4 yards

Yarn for weft: heavier and fluffier than the warp; about 15 yards of worsted weight. If the yarn is thin, it can be used two or three strands together.

This project can be made in any size. Using the dimensions listed below, students can make a 2 x 3" (5 x 8 cm) pouch or pocket. The color of the warp thread is not critical because students, again, are weaving weft-faced fabric in which the warp is almost completely covered by the weft. It is best to choose a yarn that is smooth and strong for warp. A neutral color for the warp works with any weft color.

Fourth graders wove these bags on cardboard looms. Notice how the warp thread is almost completely covered by the weft. Cotton warp, acrylic weft, approximately 2 x 3" (5 x 8 cm).

Students can weave a larger bag, using the same technique as for the small pouch. The author made this bag using two pieces of mat board, taped together at the bottom. She formed the flap by cutting the larger mat board into a point. Cotton warp, wool and chenille weft, braided and card-woven strap, 5 x 7" (13 x 18 cm).

⊞ Making the Loom

Fourth-grade students and older should be able to make this loom. Some students may need help measuring. Demonstrate each step and check students' work.

1 Mark every ¼" along both 3" (8 cm) sides of the cardboard. With scissors, cut a small line on each mark, about ½" (1 cm) long. These cuts will be the notches that hold the warp threads.

Supply students with cardboard that is thin enough to cut with scissors and will bend easily.

2 Begin winding on the warp by taping the yarn to one side of the cardboard. This will be the back.

3 Pass the thread through the first notch to the front of the loom and down to the opposite end of the cardboard. Wrap the thread through this notch to the back, through the second notch to the front, and back up to where you began.

4 Pass the thread through this second notch, to the back. Come around notch number 2, through number 3 from behind, and along the front to notches 3 and 4 on the other end. Continue winding the warp thread this way until all the notches are full. The warp should be on the front of the cardboard only. If the warp threads are on both sides of the cardboard, it is because the threads are not being brought around the notches, only through them.

Be sure students allow enough slack in the warp to prevent the cardboard from curling up. The warp thread will stretch across the front of the cardboard.

5 Tape the end of the thread to the back of the loom.

6 Once the loom is warped, fold it in half, bringing the two notched ends together with the warp threads on the outside. If a flap at the top is desired, fold the cardboard unevenly, leaving a 1–2" (3–5 cm) difference in the ends. Crease gently and secure the top edges together with a rubber band. As weaving progresses, the rubber band can be taken off.

Instruct students to curl the cardboard so that the short ends are together. Have them hold the ends in place as they pinch along the fold.

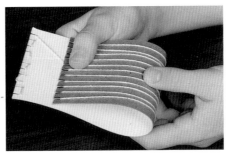

Students can create a pouch with a flap by folding the loom unevenly. Notice that the warp threads are on the outside of the loom.

A rubber band will keep the loom folded. Once students have woven an inch or so, they can remove the band.

This detail of a Mexican blanket shows weft-faced fabric woven with alternating thick and thin bands of color. Each wide band is made up of smaller bands of gradually lighter color. The shorter dashes of lighter color are woven as tapestry, with the weft yarn only woven through those warps, not from one edge to the other. Cotton warp with wool weft, from the collection of Lars Neises.

Choosing the Weft

When choosing the yarns for the weft, a variety of textures will add interest. However, too many colors and textures may create a chaotic effect. Help students choose a group of colors that harmonize. Have them test their choices by placing the yarns together in a group and examining the color combinations. Ask them to add or subtract yarns one at a time, and re-evaluate the group. Point out that using one variegated yarn will produce a striped bag without having to change threads, but using more than one variegated yarn will be too much in most projects.

The wefts should not be much longer than the width of the weaver's two outstretched arms. Have students thread the tapestry needle with the first color, pulling the end through to overlap about 6" (15 cm). Do not knot the end of the weft.

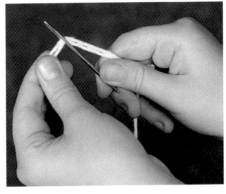

To keep the weft thread from splitting as students thread the tapestry needle, have them push a loop of yarn through the eye. Demonstrate pulling the yarn through the eye of the needle and overlapping the thread. Do not double it or knot the ends.

Weaving the Pouch

When students are ready to begin weaving, talk them through the following steps. Demonstrate as needed.

1 Begin weaving at the folded end of the loom, either the front or the back. You will be weaving both sides of this loom. Weave over one, under one across the first side. Right-handed weavers will find it easiest to weave right to left, left-handed weavers from left to right. Either way will work well as long as it's consistently done.

2 After weaving the needle across the first row on one side, pull the yarn through the warps until there is a 2" (5 cm) tail hanging down. This will be woven in later. Do not tie any knots to join wefts.

3 Turn the loom over and continue the pattern on the other side. When finished with the back, turn the loom again, and weave the second row across the front. Be sure that you are weaving the opposite pattern on the second row, going over the warps that you went under on the first row. Each time you flip the loom over, check your pattern.

4 Because there is an even number of threads on this loom, there will be a double warp thread somewhere in the project. In order to continuously weave the loom in a circle and get a plain weave pattern, there must be an odd number of warps. Because this loom is folded in half, there is always an even number of warp threads on each side. To compensate, finish one row, flip the loom over, and repeat the last pattern. If you ended under the warp, begin the next row under. This will mimic an odd number of warps, and will be almost unnoticable in the finished project.

5 Continue weaving until you run out of weft or wish to change colors.

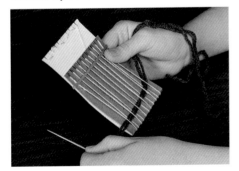

Demonstrate weaving the first row of plain weave from the folded end to the top of the cardboard loom. Leave a 2–3" (5–8 cm) tail of yarn hanging. Flip the loom over and continue weaving plain weave across these warps.

Each time students flip the loom over, they should check the first thread and proceed in the opposite pattern.

Changing Wefts

When ready, have students leave a tail hanging of the old weft and thread their needles with the new weft. This may be the same color or a new one. Instruct them to go back four wefts and weave the same over/under pattern as the row below. Explain that this will create a double weft in that area, but it will be hidden as the weaving progresses. Tell students to weave past the tail of the old weft and continue weaving around the loom as before. Change weft colors to demonstrate.

When changing wefts, there will be an area with two threads in the same pattern. This will show very little once the weft is firmly packed down. This splice allows weavers to continue the plain weave pattern with the new yarn. Tying a knot instead will usually be more visible than overlapping threads.

Weaving Weft-faced Fabric

Remind students to be very sure to pack the weft threads tightly together as they weave. The weft threads should almost completely hide the warp threads. Students can use a fork, the end of a needle, or their fingers to do this. The tighter the wefts are packed, the firmer the finished project will be. At the beginning of the project, the wefts will appear to fall off the bottom of the loom when packed tightly. This is normal. Explain to students that the wefts will begin to fill in as they continue to weave up the sides of the loom.

Show students how to create a flap on a pouch. Weave around the loom until there is no more room for wefts on the shorter side. Then, weave plain weave back and forth on one side only. Do not let this area of weaving get too narrow. The vertical stripes are created by weaving one row of a light color, followed by a row of a dark color. Repeating light, dark, light, dark over about ten rows will produce a vertical stripe. Remind students to pack their weft threads firmly.

Removing the Pouch From the Loom

Point out to students that when they get to the top of the loom, and are weaving almost on top of the notches, they are finished. To remove the pouch from the cardboard, they must bend the notches to the outside and slip the warps off. Have them pull off the tape that they used to start and end the warp. The loom should now slide out of the pouch.

Students remove the pouch from the loom by unhooking the warp threads from the notches at the top of the cardboard. They remove the tape from the inside of the loom, and weave these two warp threads into the pouch using the tapestry needle.

Finishing

Have students take a few minutes to weave the tails into the finished work. Show them how to thread the weft tail onto the needle and weave over-under into the finished fabric. Take the first tail one way and the next in the opposite direction. Weave the tails in one inch and then cut the rest off flush with the surface of the pouch. The tail at the bottom can be woven across the base of the pouch. This will help to fill in any empty warps. Sometimes turning the pouch inside-out will give a better fabric. Remind students to weave in the two cut warp ends that were taped to the loom.

Once the project is off the loom and the tails are woven in, students may wish to embellish their weavings with beads, feathers, fringe, or other ornaments. Some may want to add a strap so that the woven pouch can be worn over the head or shoulder.

Variation

Do not restrict students to weaving with only yarn. Many things can be woven into the pouch. Suggest or provide ribbon, thin fabric strips, unspun fibers, raffia or grass, audio or video tape, thin wire or metallic yarns. A few rows or sections of a pile weave (described in the frame looms chapter) also would add an interesting texture.

Ramie, or China Grass, is spun from the stem fibers of the Stingless Nettle. Sisal is made from the leaf fibers of the agave, and raffia comes from the leaves of the raffia palm.

The Complete Spinning Book
Candace Crockett

Woven Mug Rugs

Mug rugs are small pieces of fabric, woven on a cardboard loom, with the warp threads tied off at each end to prevent unravelling. They can be made any size, but these directions are for a rug about the size of a coaster. Invite students to experiment with colors and practice using a shed stick to increase weaving speed.

Vocabulary

shed, shed stick, draw-in, weft-faced, pick and pick, selvage

Materials

Each student will need:

Cardboard: a stiff piece at least 4 x 10" (10 x 25 cm)

Scissors

Tapestry needles: 2

Ruler

Pencil or pen

Metal or plastic fork

Spacer made of 2 x 6" (5 x 15 cm) strip of cardboard or heavy paper

Yarn for warp: strong and smooth, about 5 yards

Yarn for weft: various colors of a worsted weight, thicker and softer than the warp; about 8 yards

Woven by sixth graders, these mug rugs look like miniature carpets. Cotton warp, wool and acrylic weft, approximately 3 x 5" (8 x 13 cm).

Making the Loom

Follow these steps with students as you make this small version of a cardboard loom.

1 On the 4" (10 cm) sides of the cardboard, mark off ¼" (1 cm) segments. Cut about ¼" (1 cm) long slit at each mark.

2 Warp the loom by taping one end of warp thread to the back of the cardboard, then bring the thread back to the front through the first notch. Bring the thread across the front of the cardboard and through the first notch at the opposite end of the loom. From the back, bring the thread through the second notch, across the front to the second notch on the opposite end, around the back and through the third notch.

3 Continue warping back and forth until you have 16 warp threads. All the warps should be on the front of the cardboard. Cut the warp and tape the end to the back of the loom.

Using a Shed Stick

Students can use a simple trick to speed up their weaving. Show them how to weave a flat ruler over and under the warp. Then, twist the ruler onto its edge between the warps. Note that the ruler raised every other thread about 1" (3 cm) and created a triangular-shaped opening between warps. This is called a **shed**. The stick used to create the shed is called a **shed stick**.

With the stick on its side, pass the needle between the warps. Now, turn the stick flat again. Point out that the weft thread is now woven under one, over one, in the direction in which you passed the needle. Explain that, while this tool will help students weave more quickly, it will only raise one shed, or one set of threads. To weave back, turn the stick flat again and continue as before, weaving the needle over and under.

Any smooth, flat stick—such as a ruler— will work as a shed stick. A shed stick is woven over and under the warp threads.

Weaving the Mat

Demonstrate how to weave the mat. Then, circulate around the room, checking students' work and helping as necessary.

1 Begin by weaving in the 2" (5 cm) cardboard strip at the bottom of the loom to use as a spacer, indicating where to start weaving. The spacer will leave a long enough warp thread to tie in knots when the weaving is finished.

CONTINUED ON FOLLOWING PAGE

Have students insert a piece of folded paper or lightweight cardboard through the shed at the bottom of the loom.

2 Choose the first weft color and thread the tapestry needle with a one-yard length. Do not tie a knot in the weft, just bring the tail through the needle until it overlaps about 2" (5 cm).

3 Begin weaving by turning the shed stick on its side to raise every other warp. Pass the needle through the open shed. Pull the rest of the weft through, stopping with a 2–3" (5–8 cm) long tail. Turn the shed stick flat and weave back in the opposite direction, making sure that the over/under pattern is opposite on the second row.

4 Continue weaving until 6" (15 cm) of yarn is left on the needle. Leave a tail hanging of the old weft and thread your needle with the new weft. This may be the same color or a new one. Begin weaving with the new weft on the other side of the warp. If you ended with the old weft on the left, begin the new weft from the right. When the weaving is finished, use the tapestry needle to weave these ends back into the fabric 1–2" (3–5 cm).

Most people are either right or left-handed, and can weave fastest from the side of their dominant hand. For example, right-handed people usually weave faster from right to left. Suggest that students use a shed stick to weave with their slower hand, and weave back with their faster hand.

This detail of a modern rug from India shows bright colors and a simple weave structure. In the solid blue bands at the top and bottom, you can see a twill weave; the rest of the rug is a plain weave, weft-faced fabric. Cotton warp and weft, from the collection of Jane Schelly.

⧉ Avoiding Draw-in

As students weave, remind them to pack the weft threads down with a fork, needle, or their fingers until the weft threads almost completely hide the warp threads. The firmer the wefts are packed, the firmer the finished project will be.

Students may notice the sides of their weaving starting to pull in, making the fabric narrower. This is called **draw-in** and is caused by pulling the weft too tightly across the fabric. This is a challenge that all beginning weavers face. To correct draw-in, leave an arc of weft across the warp, rather than bringing it straight across. Watch the edges and leave more of an arc if the edges begin to draw-in.

Explain to students that these right and left edges of the fabric are called the **selvage**. Selvage edges are where

the weft threads wrap around the warps. There's no loose end of yarn to unravel on these edges. Have them look at commercially made fabric and note the selvage, or the edge that does not unravel.

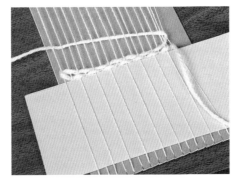

Caution students to watch the last few threads on each side of the weaving. If these threads begin to pull towards the center, the fabric will begin to narrow. This is called draw-in, and is very hard to correct once it has begun.

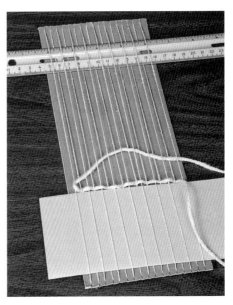

Students can avoid draw-in by leaving an arc of weft yarn each time they weave across the warp. Explain that the weft does not simply go between the warp, but must be long enough to travel over and under each of the warps.

⧉ Using Color for Stripes

Students will learn quickly that, by changing the color of their weft yarn, they can weave a horizontal stripe into their fabric. Point out that they can also weave vertical stripes and even checks into weft-faced fabric if they are careful to pack the wefts down tightly on top of each other.

To weave vertical stripes, students will need two colors of weft. The more contrast between the two colors, the better the stripe. They also will need a second tapestry needle.

Demonstrate alternating the two weft colors, one row after another to create a vertical stripe. Weave color A, then B, then repeat A B A B A B. One color will always weave under

This is a classic example of Mexican blanket weaving with brightly colored stripes, alternately thin and thick, and subtle gradations of value and color within wider bands. The weaver created the thin stripe with the diamond pattern by skipping over groups of warp threads rather than weaving over one, under one. Cotton warp and weft, from the collection of Lars Neises.

the even number warps; the second will always weave under the odd number warps. This is called weaving **pick and pick.**

To create a checkered pattern, weave colors A B A B A B as before, then switch the sequence: A B A B A B B A B A B A. The wefts will appear to switch places, and create a checkerboard effect.

Pick-and-pick stripes are an easy way to create bold geometric designs. Diagonal lines move across the width of these tapestry belts from Guatemala, making triangles and diamonds. The details are possible in these small bands because of the small scale of all the threads. The weft is the size of embroidery floss. Cotton warp and weft, 1" (3 cm) wide, collection of the author.

⊞ Finishing

Have students continue weaving in desired colors until the fabric measures 4" (10 cm) long. Then, have them cut the warp off the loom by the notches at each end. Demonstrate pulling out the cardboard spacer and tying 8 knots on each side, using an overhand knot with 2 warps at a time. Trim the warp fringe to the desired length.

Remind students to take a few minutes to weave the tails into their finished work. They should thread the weft tail onto the needle and weave over/under into the finished fabric about 1" (3 cm), then cut the rest of the weft off flush with the surface of the fabric.

Show students how to rewarp the loom and weave a second mat. Explain that, if they use the same colors, the mats will look like a set, even if they change the pattern of stripes in each mat. This will allow students to experiment and still end up with a set of mats.

When finished, press each mat with an iron and a damp cloth. This will even out the surface and greatly improve the final product.

Show students how to use a paper clip or tapestry needle to slide the loop of a knot into just the right position.

Tapestry Picture

Once students have mastered the basic skills for weaving on a cardboard loom, they can move on to weaving pictures in their fabric. **Tapestry** is a version of plain weave in which different color wefts share the same row. Fabrics made in this way are called tapestries.

Vocabulary

weft-face, tapestry, shed stick, cartoon

Materials

Each student will need:

Cardboard: a stiff piece at least 6 x 10" (15 x 25 cm). The loom should be the size of the finished tapestry.

Scissors

Tapestry needles: one for each color weft

Ruler

Pencil

Metal or plastic fork

Yarn for warp: strong and smooth, about 12 yards

Yarn for weft: various colors of a worsted weight, thicker and softer than the warp; about 60 yards for a 6 x 10" (15 x 25 cm) tapestry

Tapestry design

Stick: smooth and flat, slightly longer than the width of tapestry

A fifth grader wove this tapestry of her house. She stitched on the roof line, red flowers, and the window and door details after finishing the tapestry. *House on Madison*, cotton warp, acrylic weft, 6 x 7½" (15 x 19 cm).

Note how the roof lines of these small houses stand out clearly against the white background and the sides of the houses blend into the grey of the foreground. Woven in Argentina, cotton warp, wool weft, 5 x 7" (13 x 18 cm), from the collection of Kay Hathhorn.

▦ Designing the Tapestry

Simple, bold shapes work well for this project. Have students cut out paper that is the same size and shape as their looms. Have them sketch their designs in pencil first, then darken the main shapes with a bold permanent marker. Explain that tapestry artists use such line drawings, or **cartoons,** as guides while weaving.

Have students design the color scheme for their pictures with colored pencils or crayons. Discuss with students how yarns that have contrast in color or value (the relative lightness or darkness of the color) will help the background look as if it is behind the subject of the picture.

For their first designs, suggest that students weave an area of ½" (1 cm) or more at the bottom of their pictures that is all one color. This will allow them to weave all the way across the warp without changing color, and will establish strong foundations for their tapestries.

Animals, insects, and fish are wonderful subjects for tapestry. Have students simplify the shape, and keep the main subjects large. Here, the bright yellow stands out against the blue water, and is repeated in a border. Polish tapestry wall hanging, linen warp, wool weft, 15 x 15" (38 x 38 cm), collection of Ruth Beal.

Making the Loom

Review with students how to make a cardboard loom and set up the warp. Have students tape their designs on the cardboard before warping their looms. Suggest that they use a shed stick on this project to speed up their weaving. As they get to the end of the project, however, they will not have room for the shed stick and will have to resume weaving with a needle.

Have students darken the lines of their cartoons with permanent markers, then tape their cartoons to cardboard looms before they begin warping.

Stylized birds show up boldly on this cream background. Many of the Central American countries produce small, simple tapestries for the tourist and export trade. These nicely woven and inexpensive weavings will help your students understand how a tapestry is made. Woven in Peru, cotton warp, wool weft, 15 x 15" (38 x 38 cm), collection of the author.

⊞ Weaving the Tapestry

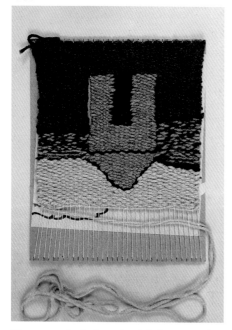

Weave a sample tapestry, joining several color areas with different methods. Show students the different edges that result. Here, you can see the sharp color changes on the sides of the house, and the open slit formed by slit weave. The front door has a less distinct shape, and illustrates the saw-tooth effect of dovetailing. The hills behind the house are woven with weft of two different colors, twisted together.

Demonstrate these steps for students. Check their understanding of the concepts of background and foreground and the tapestry joining techniques. You may need to provide assistance as students weave their own tapestries.

1 Begin weaving your background color across all the warps for ½" (1 cm) or more. When you reach the first shape, bring the background color to the front of the warp and continue across the warp with the next color. Cut another weft thread of the background color and use it to continue the other side of the design.

2 There are two ways of joining areas of colors: **slit weaving** and **dovetailing.** The slit weaving technique produces a sharp color change and crisp, geometric shapes. It is called slit weaving because it forms an opening, or slit, between areas of color in the woven fabric. The slits can be sewn closed in the finished tapestry, but they are commonly left as they are woven. The dovetailing tech-

nique interlocks colors by having the two wefts share a warp thread. This produces a saw-tooth edge between areas of color. Be sure to pack the weft thread down firmly. Tapestries are weft-faced fabrics.

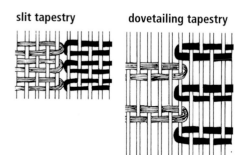

slit tapestry   dovetailing tapestry

3 Follow your cartoon for the placement of colors in your design. Be sure to watch for excessive draw-in on the selvages.

⊞ Removing the Tapestry from the Loom

Once the picture is completely woven, and all the wefts are firmly packed, students can remove their tapestries from the cardboard. After the weaving is off the loom, the side with the cut yarns becomes the back of the picture. Most tapestry weavers leave the tails hanging; cutting them short increases the chance that the tails will work their way through to the front of the weaving. If you prefer to leave students' tapestries on the cardboard looms, using them to display the tapestries, have students weave in all the cut ends with the tapestry needle.

There are several ways to mount students' tapestry weavings for display.

• If you have removed the cardboard, you can slide small dowels through the loops at the top and bottom. This will give the fabric weight at the bottom edge and help it to hang straight.

• Consider stitching the finished tapestries to a larger piece of commercial fabric. Use a firmly woven fabric to support the weight of the weaving. Frame or stretch this over a wooden picture frame.

• Suggest that students embroider small details on top of their weavings. This will allow them to add small areas of color that would be difficult to weave into their pictures.

Rag Place Mats

With the same kind of cardboard loom as before, students can make larger projects. Using strips of fabric for weft will help the weaving on this place mat go quickly.

Vocabulary

shed, shed stick, draw-in, weft-faced, pick and pick, selvage

Materials

Each student will need:

Cardboard: a stiff piece, about 12 x 18" (30 x 46 cm)

Scissors

Mat knife (optional, might be needed for very heavy cardboard)

Tapestry needles

Ruler

Pencil or pen

Metal or plastic fork

Yarn for warp: strong and smooth, about 24 yards

Rags for weft: 1 yard of lightweight cotton or cotton/polyester cut or ripped into strips about ½–1" (1–3 cm) wide.

Stick: smooth and flat, slightly longer than the width of place mat

Most lightweight cotton and cotton blend fabrics are easily torn into strips. Make a cut on the selvage the width of the desired weft strips. The heavier the fabric, the thinner the strips need to be.

Grip each side of the cut and pull the fabric apart firmly. Once you have torn the fabric to the other selvage, cut the reinforced edge with scissors.

Strips of rags weave quickly into a large place mat. A sixth grader wove this mat, combining solid color and print fabrics in the weft. Cotton warp, cotton-poly rags for weft, 12 x 18" (30 x 46 cm).

This rag weave fabric was produced in Canada as yardage. The fabric could be cut and used for rugs, curtains, or garments. Cotton warp, rag weft, from the collection of Ruth Beal.

⊞ Making the Loom

See the mug rug lesson to review directions on making a cardboard loom and setting up the warp. The steps are the same for all cardboard looms; only the weight of the cardboard varies. This project uses very heavy cardboard because of the size of the weaving. You may need to use a mat knife to cut the slits at the ends of the loom for young students. Older students should not use a mat knife without adult supervision.

Weaving the Place Mat

Students can thread the rag strips onto the tapestry needle for this project, or they might find it just as easy to weave the rags using only their fingers.

Have them weave the place mat in plain weave, as they wove the mug rug, weaving from edge to edge, taking care to avoid draw-in. If students wish to use a shed stick, they will need something longer than a ruler. Provide flat, smooth sticks that are two or more inches longer than the width of the looms.

Instruct students to continue to weave plain weave until they can't fit any more wefts across the warp. Remind them to pack the wefts tightly to create a good, firm mat. It is sometimes easier to weave half of the mat and then start at the other end, meeting in the center.

Any of the color and stripe techniques that students used in the last few projects will also work well in rag weaving. Suggest that they consider weaving both horizontal and vertical stripes in their place mats. They can also use printed fabric as weft for a different look.

To change weft strips, leave tails of rags on each end of the weft strip to be woven in later, or overlap two strips of weft to continue the pattern. The old weft and the new one will be in the same shed for about 2" (5 cm). Cut the tails off, even with the surface of the fabric.

Remind students to always leave an arc of weft to prevent draw-in on their fabric.

Show students how to pack the weft strips in firmly with a fork. Suggest that using a shed stick for this project may speed up their weaving.

Finishing

Have students take the finished mat off the loom by removing the warp threads from around the notches at each end. Remind them to take a few minutes to weave the tails into their finished work by threading the weft tail onto the needle and weaving over and under into the finished fabric about one inch. Then, have them cut the rest of the weft flush with the surface of the fabric.

Students can now rewarp the loom and weave a second mat. When they are finished, press each mat with an iron and a damp cloth. This will even out the surface and greatly improve the final product.

Math

Students can estimate the total amount of yarn used for warp. Adapt for addition or multiplication problems.

Social Studies

Contact local farms to arrange a visit during April or May to see sheep shearing. Many ranchers will donate a small amount of raw (unprocessed) fleece to teachers. Students can try spinning the fleece by twirling the wool fibers between their fingers. If fleece is not available, use cotton balls. Be sure students tease the fibers apart before spinning them.

Environmental Science

Have students include natural and recycled materials, such as audio and video tape, plant leaves, grasses, and thin twigs, in their weavings. Try assigning some students to gather materials from the natural world and some to gather human-made materials. Ask students to predict how each group will differ, and then compare the finished projects of both groups. Discuss how the resources in an area can influence the look of items produced there.

Writing/Communications

For the rag place mat, have students collect old or worn-out clothing from their family and cut them into strips. After they have woven their mats, they can write or tell the story of who owned the fabrics, or what was special about one color or pattern in their weaving. Talk to the class about quilting and the practice of recycling worn fabrics into new items.

A wide range of projects can be made on cardboard looms. Once students have mastered warping the cardboard, they can vary the size of the project to suit their interests.

One of the softest animal fibers is the undercoat of the musk ox. The Eskimos of Alaska call it *Quiviet*. It is thinner in diameter than the finest cashmere. The musk oxen shed this hair each year, so no sheering is needed. The fiber is gathered from wild herds as it falls to the ground, or is caught on branches. Quiviet from domesticated herds is combed, and the fiber spun into fine yarn for knitting.

CHAPTER 3

Frame Looms

Frame looms are more rigid and permanent than cardboard looms. They can be any size, from the small one used in these lessons to the large rug looms used by Navaho weavers. If they are made well, they can last many years. In the following projects, students will learn several new weaving patterns and techniques that will help them weave with greater speed. (Note: Although the lessons in this chapter call for frame looms, students also can use heavy cardboard looms.)

Hsi-Ling Shih was a Chinese empress who, legend says, invented sericulture, the art of raising silk worms for spinning and weaving, and taught these skills to her people.

The New Book of Goddesses and Heroines
Patricia Monaghan

This is an example of the beautiful woven decorations used in India. This tasseled fabric hangs in front of the camel's knees and the tassels move about as the camel walks. Pile weave, wool warp and weft, approximately 12 x 12" (30 x 30 cm), from the collection of Jane Schelly.

Rya and Tapestry Sampler

Rya is a **pile weave** technique used in tapestries and rugs. It produces a tufted effect on the top of the fabric, using short lengths of yarn that are knotted around the warps between rows of plain weave. In this project, students create a mini-sampler of the rya and tapestry techniques. Once complete, they can sew the sampler together to form a small pouch, combine it with other fabric in a larger project, or display it flat.

Vocabulary

shed, shed stick, heddle rod, mock tapestry, clasped weft, pick and pick, pile weave, rya knots

Materials

See page 88 for instructions on building a frame loom.

Each student will need:

Frame loom or cardboard loom
Tapestry needles: large-eyed, 1–2
Scissors
Plastic or metal fork
Masking tape
Stick: smooth and flat to use as a
    shed stick (i.e., a ruler)
Dowel, chopstick, or pencil: about
    10" (25 cm) long
String for heddles: smooth, very
    thin, and strong, about 1 yard
String for warp: strong and
    smooth, about 5 yards
Yarn for weft: softer and thicker
    than the warp yarn, about 6 yards
    of 3–5 colors; small lengths of
    yarn, at least 12" (30 cm) long.
    Thin yarns may be doubled,
    tripled, or mixed with other yarns
    to make a good thickness.

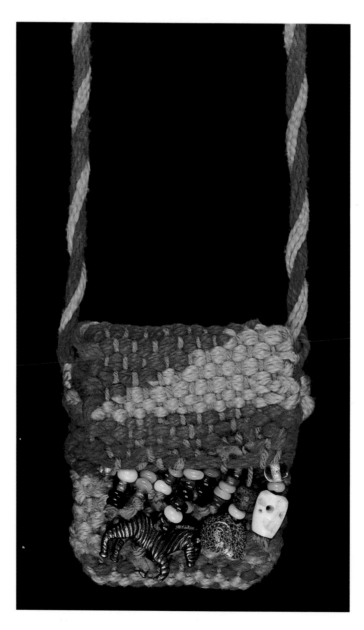

Once the fabric is off the loom, the warp threads can be threaded with beads, shells, or charms to create a fringe. Cotton warp and weft, woven by the author.

Knotted pile weaves create intricate designs. Detail of a pile weave saddlebag from India, wool warp and weft, from the collection of Jane Schelly.

⊞ Setting up the Loom

Show students how to warp a frame loom by following these steps.

1 Using the warp thread, begin by finding the center ten nails on the top and bottom of the frame loom. If you are not using the entire width of the loom, it is best to center the project as best you can. Approximate centering is all that's needed, just enough to equalize the tension on the loom.

2 Tie one end of the warp thread to the first nail you are using. Take the warp to the corresponding nail on the opposite end of the frame. Wrap the thread around that nail and return along the front of the frame to the other end. Continue to wrap the thread around the nails, going back and forth, until you have 20 warp threads. The warp will be on the front of the frame.

3 Tie off the warp thread around the nail.

If students will be using all the nails on the frame, have them start at one end and warp until all the nails are full. If students will not need all the nails, have them count out from the middle of the frame loom to center their warp threads.

Show students how to wind the warp thread back and forth around the nails and tie a knot in the warp around the last nail needed.

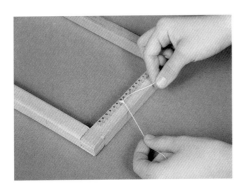

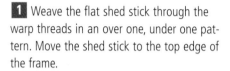 ## Using a Shed Stick and Heddle Rod

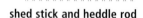

On this project, students will be using a shed stick and heddle rod to separate the warp threads for weaving. Demonstrate this technique as follows.

shed stick and heddle rod

1 Weave the flat shed stick through the warp threads in an over one, under one pattern. Move the shed stick to the top edge of the frame.

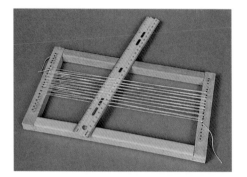

Have students weave their shed sticks over and under the warps, and then slide them to one end of the frame.

2 To raise the opposite set of warp threads, creating a different shed, make a heddle rod from the dowel and string. Center the dowel over the warps. Tie the heddle string onto the dowel at the left edge of the warp and thread the other end through the tapestry needle.

Adding the heddle rod is easier if a second person holds it in place as students pick up the set of threads not raised by the shed stick. Be sure students take the thread under the desired warp and then over the heddle rod.

3 Raise the dowel about 1" (2 cm) above the warp threads and loop the heddle string under the first warp thread that you want to raise. This will depend on the placement of the shed stick. You want the heddle rod to raise the opposite set of warps as the shed stick. If the shed stick is under the first warp, loop the heddle string under the second.

4 After you loop under the first warp, come back around the top of the dowel. Now loop around the second warp you want to raise.

5 Continue across the width of the warp. When you reach the other side, tie off the heddle string on the dowel.

6 If there are some heddle strings that are longer than others, take a moment to even them out. Once they are all about the same length, place a piece of tape over the top of the dowel to keep them from shifting as you weave.

Be sure students secure the string heddles with a piece of tape.

Pulling up on the heddle rod will allow students to slide their weft through the shed. Check that students' heddle rods are held away from their shed sticks.

7 The heddle rod will work best if you move it away from the shed stick. Move it to the center of the warp and gently pull it up, away from the warp. It will raise the opposite set of threads from the shed stick. You are now ready to weave.

Turning the shed stick on edge raises the opposite shed from the heddle rod. Students can now weave back and forth without having to count over and under.

Weaving

Invite students to choose colors and textures for their weavings. They should use at least three different colors, but one or two more will work if they all harmonize. Have students begin weaving as before, with a small tail left at the start. Circulate among students, making sure they have used shed sticks to raise one shed and heddle rods to raise the other shed correctly. Students are now ready to weave plain weave without having to count over one, under one. This will greatly speed up their weaving.

Demonstrate the following steps to weave a rya and tapestry sampler.

1 Weave one color in plain weave for 1" (3 cm). Set the first color down at one side, with the needle still on it. Weave one row of plain weave with a second color, leaving a tail at the side of the weaving. Alternate colors one row after another. This is called weaving **pick and pick.** If the weft rows are packed down firmly, this will form vertical stripes. Continue weaving pick and pick for ½" (1 cm).

2 The next section is a **mock tapestry** technique called **clasped weft.** This looks like traditional tapestry, where there is more than one weft color in a horizontal row, but is much faster and simpler.

For this section, there are two weft threads in each row. One color weft will start from the right, another color will start from the left.

When they meet in the middle, they will lock around each other and exit the way they entered. This will give a double weft in that row. Once the two yarns are clasped in the middle, a gentle pull to the left or right will move the joint and create an interesting shape as you weave.

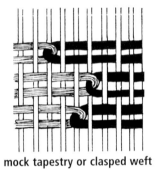

mock tapestry or clasped weft

Creating designs is easy with clasped wefts. Demonstrate by inserting the weft as usual through one of the sheds. Leave this shed open.

Once you are on the opposite side of the fabric, loop the needle under your second weft color. Return through the same open shed, dragging the second color with you.

Once the two wefts are interlocked, pull them back and forth in the shed to position them.

When the wefts are in the desired position, pack them down firmly.

CONTINUED ON FOLLOWING PAGE

The simplest way to weave clasped weft on a small frame loom is to bring one weft all the way through the shed, loop it around the second color weft, and return it through the same shed. Keep the shed open and drag the second color part way into the warp. Gently pull the wefts right or left to place the colors. Close the shed and pack the wefts into place. Repeat this until you have about 1½" (4 cm) of clasped weft.

4 Repeat the pick and pick design for ½" (1 cm).

5 Weave two rows of plain weave with one color.

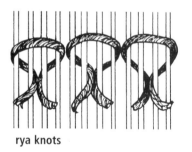

rya knots

6 To make the rya knot diamond, tie a 2–3" (5–8 cm) long piece of yarn around the center 4 warp threads. Weave 2 rows of plain weave. Tie 3 rya knots using the center 12 threads, 4 warp threads per knot. Weave 2 rows of plain weave. Tie 5 rya knots across all the warps, 4 warp threads per knot. Weave 2 rows of plain weave. Tie 3 knots on the center 12 warps. Weave 2 rows of plain weave. End the pile weave section with 1 knot on the center 4 warps. Weave 2 rows of plain weave. Trim the rya knots to the desired length.

7 Weave your choice of pick and pick, solid color plain weave, or horizontal stripes until the weaving measures 5" (13 cm).

This finished sampler shows solid color at the bottom, followed by pick and pick, clasped weft, pick and pick, rya knots, and solid color finishing off the top.

Finishing

Have students remove the fabric from the frame loom by cutting the warp threads next to the nails. Have them tie every two warp threads in an overhand knot as close to the last weft row as possible, and gently remove the other end of the fabric from the frame. Then students can weave in any tails and sew the sides together to form a pouch or anything else they desire. Students might thread beads onto the warp threads before trimming them short.

Once off the loom, students tie the warp in pairs, close to the last row of weft. They will only need to tie off the top edge, since the bottom edge was woven next to the warp loops. Have them weave in the two warps that were tied around the nails at the beginning and end of the warp.

Balanced Plain Weave Fabric

For this project, students will be using the same yarn for both warp and weft. The goal is to weave a balanced plain weave fabric that has the same number of threads in one inch of warp as in one inch of weft. The weft-faced projects students have completed previously were rather stiff and firm. This balanced fabric will be more like the kind of fabric used for garments. By using one color of warp and a different color of weft, students can observe how colors can be blended together in weaving.

Vocabulary
shed, shed stick, heddle rod, balanced plain weave

Materials
See page 88 for instructions on building a frame loom.

Each student will need:
Frame loom or cardboard loom
Tapestry needle: large-eyed
Scissors
Plastic or metal fork
Masking tape
Shed stick: a smooth flat stick
  (i.e., a ruler)
Dowel, chopstick, or pencil: about
  10" (25 cm) long
String for heddles: very thin,
  smooth, and strong, about 1 yard
Yarn for warp and weft: knitting
  worsted weight, variety of complementary colors. Check the
  diameter of the yarn by wrapping
  it around a ruler. With the yarn
  just touching, but not crowded
  together, there should be 16–20
  wraps in 1" (3 cm). If there are
  less than 16, the yarn is too thick
  for this project. If there are more
  than 20, the yarn is too thin.

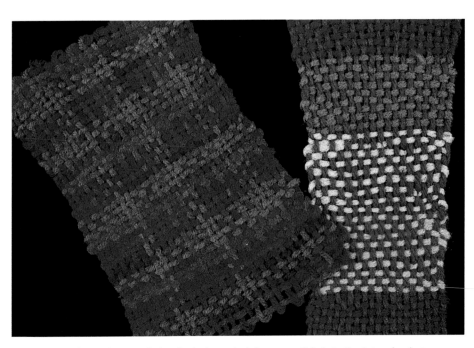

The distinguishing characteristic of a balanced plain weave fabric is the interplay between the colors in the warp and the colors in the weft. These examples, woven by sixth graders, show how weft color can affect the warp. The fabric on the left is woven from a variegated yarn in both the warp and the weft, creating a random plaid effect. The fabric on the right has a blue warp and different weft stripes. Acrylic warp and weft.

A great way to learn about color interaction in weaving is to make a color sampler. This example has black, white, red, yellow, and blue warp stripes. The colors are repeated in the weft so that the secondary color emerges where the two primary colors intersect. The black and white areas show how color is lightened or darkened. Woven by the author, wool warp and weft.

Using the color wheel will help students choose compatible warp and weft colors. Choosing two primary colors—red, blue, or yellow—will produce a secondary color—green, orange, or purple—in the finished weaving. Choosing two complementary colors, however, will produce a muddy, brown fabric.

Setting up the Loom and Weaving the Fabric

Review the directions in the rya and tapestry section on setting up a frame loom. This weaving can be as wide as the loom. Have students increase the number of threads on their looms as desired.

Have students begin by turning the shed stick to open the first shed, inserting the weft, and leaving a tail. Remind them to use a fork or their fingers to pack the weft in place. Then, have them raise the heddle rod, insert the weft, and, again, pack the weft.

Students will be weaving plain weave again, but the challenge in this project is to get a feel for how firmly to pack the weft threads. After students have woven eight rows, have them use a ruler to measure the fabric. If they have less than 1" (3 cm), they are packing too hard; more than 1" (3 cm), and they are packing too loosely. Advise them to adjust their packing and continue to weave.

Suggest that students change weft colors to observe the way different colors combine in a balanced weave. As they are weaving, caution them to leave an arc in the weft to avoid having the fabric draw-in.

Advise students to be very careful as they pack in each weft row. They should place the weft lightly, and not pack it firmly as in the weft-faced projects.

As students weave, remind them to keep an arc on their wefts to prevent draw-in. Point out that you can see the warp thread, as well as the weft threads, on this fabric.

Finishing

Have students continue weaving as far as possible. Then, have them cut the warp ends at the top, by the nails, and tie every two warps close to the last weft. Tell them to gently remove the other end of the fabric from the frame, and weave in any tails. The fabric will look much better if gently washed by hand, laid flat to dry, then pressed with an iron and a damp cloth.

Students can rewarp their looms and weave several fabric swatches that can be sewn together to form a larger piece of cloth.

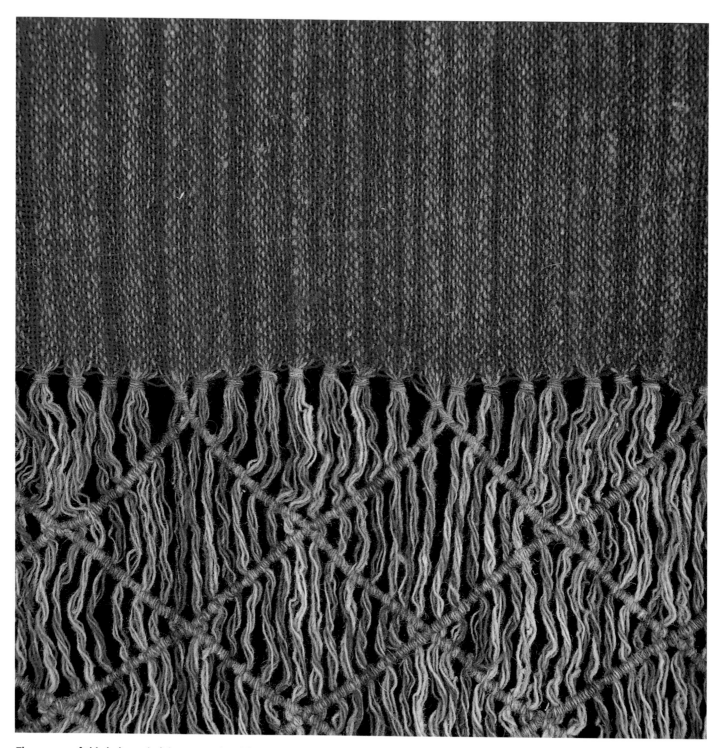

The weave of this balanced plain weave shawl from Mexico shows
pink, orange, red, and brown stripes in the warp and a red weft.
The long warp threads are knotted into an intricate pattern called
"Mexican fringe." Wool warp and weft, from the collection of Sue
Ellen Heflin.

Balanced Plain Weave, Plaid

Students can now weave another balanced plain weave fabric, but with a stripe pattern in the warp which will be repeated in the weft. This will make a plaid pattern. Have students continue to balance the number of warp threads and the number of weft rows.

Vocabulary
shed, shed stick, heddle rod, balanced plain weave, plaid, tartan

Materials
See page 88 for instructions on building a frame loom.

Each student will need:
Frame or cardboard loom
Tapestry needle: large-eyed
Scissors
Plastic or metal fork
Masking tape
Shed stick: any smooth flat stick
   (i.e., a ruler)
Dowel, chopstick, or pencil: about
   10" (25 cm) long
String for heddles: very thin,
   smooth, and strong, about 1 yard
Yarn for warp and weft: knitting
   worsted weight, various colors.
   Check the diameter of the yarn by
   wrapping it around a ruler. With
   the yarn just touching, but not
   crowded together, there should be
   16–20 wraps in one inch. If there
   are less than 16, the yarn is too
   thick for this project. If there are
   more than 20, the yarn is too
   thin.

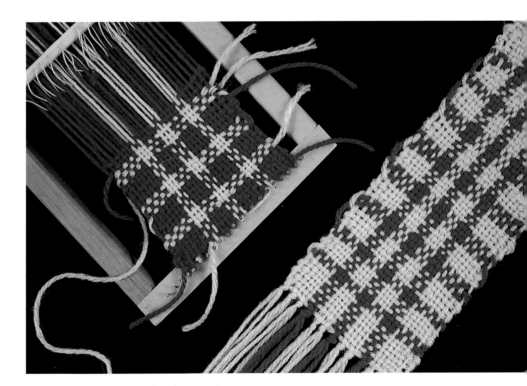

Weaving with just two colors is a good way to start learning about plaids. Once students are comfortable weaving plaids, they can add more colors and create more complex stripes. Plaid fabrics woven by a sixth grade student, acrylic warp and weft.

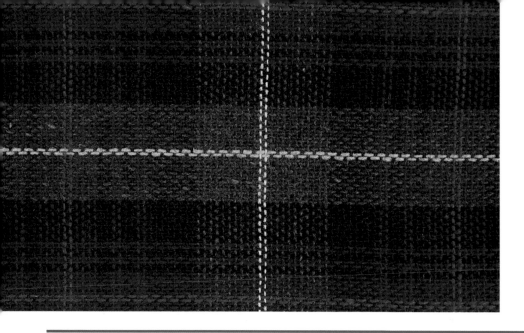

In this detail of commercial plaid fabric, plain weave, the light stripe is visually dominant over the wider, dark stripes. The black, blue, red, green, and yellow warp and weft colors are all clearly visible in this balanced plain weave. Acrylic wool blend warp and weft.

Designing the Plaid

Before warping the frame loom, it is a good idea for students to plan their stripe patterns on a sample board. Limit students to no more than three colors for the first plaid. More than three colors will be very hard to weave. Have them wind the warp threads around a scrap of cardboard or heavy paper in the order they plan to use them in the plaid. Ask them how the colors look together. Is there one color that is too strong or too weak? Suggest that they add or subtract colors. Encourage them to wind several arrangements of colors before choosing the pattern for the warp.

Ask students to note how light colors tend to come forward, while dark colors tend to recede. Point out that a narrow stripe of a light color will seem as strong as a wide area of a dark color.

Students can plan their plaids on small scraps of cardboard. Have them wrap the colors in different sequences to see if they prefer regular repeats, or less formal, irregular color repeats. Remind students that only one row of a color will create a dotted line in the fabric as the color disappears under the other threads.

Once students decide on a stripe sequence, they can wind the warp on the loom.

Setting up the Loom and Using a Shed Stick and Heddle Rod

As before, have students tie one end of the warp thread to the first nail they are using. Instruct them to take the warp to the corresponding nail on the opposite end of the frame, wrap the warp around that nail, and return to the other side. Have them continue to wrap the warp around the nails, changing colors to match their stripe samples. Students should wrap from one side of the frame to the other, until they have the pattern they want in the warp threads. Then, they can tie off the warp threads around the nail.

Review with students the directions for using a shed stick and heddle rod in the section on rya and tapestry.

Tartans are plaid fabrics that are associated with the clans of Scotland. This is a detail of the McKenzie tartan. Note the diagonal line formed by the twill weave structure. A tartan fabric should have a 45° angle to the twill line.

Weaving the Fabric

Advise students to begin weaving as they did for their balanced plain weave fabric. (See page 43.) Remind them to pack the weft so that eight rows measure one inch.

For their plaid weave, tell students to keep track of the order of the stripes in the warp, matching them in the weft. If they have very small spaces between where a weft color stops and where it starts again, caution students not to cut it and restart. If there is less than two inches between rows, have them carry the color along the edge of the fabric. If students intend to sew the finished fabric into a wallet, purse, or garment, the selvages will likely be hidden in the seams, hiding the weft threads carried on the edge of the plaid.

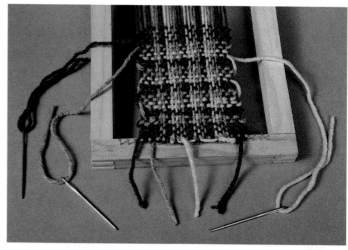

To create a plaid fabric, students weave the same colors, in the same sequence, in the weft as in the warp. This repetition of the stripe in both directions creates a plaid fabric. Students weave tails in later. If there is a short distance between colors, students can carry the unused weft colors along the edge of the fabric.

Finishing

Have students continue weaving as far as possible. Then, have them cut the warp ends at the top, by the nails, and tie every two warps close to the last weft. Tell them to gently remove the other end of the fabric from the frame, and weave in any tails. The fabric will look much better if gently washed by hand, laid flat to dry, then pressed with an iron and a damp cloth.

To create fabric with finished edges on all four sides, have students remove the shed stick and heddle rod and, with a needle, weave the remaining warp to the very top of the loom. Then, students can unhook the warps at the top and bottom.

Anytime that you make a stripe pattern in the warp, and repeat that same color sequence in the weft, you will have a plaid. But any plaid is not a tartan. The word *tartan* refers specifically to plaid fabrics that have been registered with the Scottish Tartan Society. This group, established in 1963, records and recognizes the official weaving patterns of the traditional clans of Scotland. Each clan has one or more official tartans, with the colors, sequence, and number of threads specified. Traditional tartans are woven in a twill weave, with the twill line forming a perfect 45° angle in the color squares.

Balanced Plain Weave, Log Cabin

Log cabin weave has a "color weave effect," meaning that there is an interplay between the colors of the thread and the weave structure. Although students are still weaving a simple balanced plain weave fabric, the color sequence of the warp and weft create the illusion of a complex cloth.

Vocabulary

shed, shed stick, heddle rod, balanced plain weave, log cabin, color weave effect

Materials

See page 88 for instructions on building a frame loom.

Each student will need:

Frame or cardboard loom

Tapestry needle: large-eyed

Scissors

Plastic or metal fork

Masking tape

Shed stick: any smooth flat stick (i.e., a ruler)

Dowel, chopstick, or pencil: about 10" (25 cm) long

String for heddles: very thin, smooth, and strong; about 1 yard

Yarn for warp and weft: knitting worsted weight, two colors for the warp and the same colors for the weft, about 10 yards of each color (for 5 x 10"; 13 x 25 cm fabric). Check the diameter of the yarn by wrapping it around a ruler. With the yarn just touching, but not crowded together, there should be 16–20 wraps in 1" (3 cm). If there are less than 16, the yarn is too thick for this project. If there are more than 20, the yarn is too thin.

Plain weave can appear very complex once you master the log cabin pattern. This fabric, woven by a sixth grader, alternates between horizontal and vertical stripes. Acrylic warp and weft.

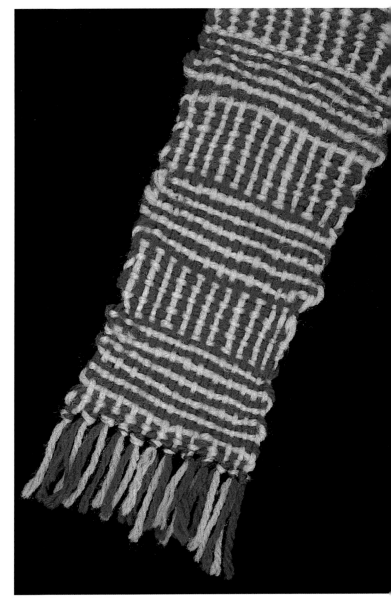

Log Cabin Weave

Students can create an interesting pattern by weaving light and dark threads in the warp and weft of a balanced plain weave fabric. The complex look of the cloth is an optical illusion created by the intersection of light and dark threads.

Log cabin weave needs a contrast in the two colors to be effective. Two similar colors, such as white and light yellow, will not show the optical illusion typical of log cabin. In this example, there are two blue threads alternating with two black threads. Detail of log cabin weave fabric used for place mats, woven by the author, cotton warp and weft.

Setting up the Loom and Using a Shed Stick and Heddle Rod

Have students begin by tying one of their threads to the first nail on the loom. Have them wrap the thread around the first and second nails on the opposite end of the frame. Tell them to skip a space, leaving it for the other warp color, and continue in this manner across the width of the loom. Students should tie the warp thread to the last nail.

Have students tie their second warp color onto the second nail on one end of the loom. Instruct them to wind the warp, filling in the spaces they left in the first color. Again, they should tie the warp thread to the last nail.

Review with students the directions for using a shed stick and heddle rod in the section on rya and tapestry.

The warp for log cabin weave needs to have a light and dark pattern in the threads. Wind the first color of the warp around the first and second nails on the loom, then the third and fourth nails, and so on. Wind the second color around the second and third nails, then the fourth and fifth nails, and so on. The two colors will then alternate in the warp.

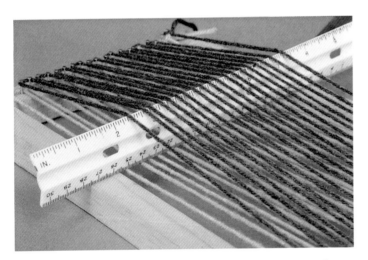

The alternating light and dark threads of the warp will mean that one shed will have all dark threads.

It is easy to pick up the second shed, since the colors in the warp contrast. You will have a dark shed, and a light shed.

⧉ Weaving the Fabric

In the first weft row, students should be careful to keep the warps in a consistent light/dark order. The log cabin pattern is created, as with the plaid pattern, by repeating the color sequence of the warp in the weft. With a light and dark sequence in the warp, and a light and dark sequence in the weft, students will see a pronounced vertical stripe appear. As long as they continue weaving light and dark, the stripe will continue.

When weaving the plaid pattern, students tried to faithfully repeat the warp order in the weft. However, in the log cabin pattern, they can experiment with that order to create a variety of horizontal and vertical stripes. If they want to change the direction of the stripe, all they need to do is repeat one of the threads. Instead of weaving light, dark, light, dark, and so on, they weave light, dark, dark, light, dark, light, thus throwing off the sequence. This will reverse the color order in the weft and change the direction of the stripe.

As in weaving plaid, students will repeat the color sequence of the warp when they weave the weft. In log cabin, this produces a dramatic stripe effect. Remind students not to pack the weft in too tightly, and to leave an arc in their weft to avoid draw-in.

To change the direction of the stripe from horizontal to vertical, repeat one of the colors in the weft. This will reverse the color sequence, and change the pattern.

The diamond is the Mayan symbol for the universe and is woven into the clothing of their descendants, the people of Chiapas, Mexico, and Guatemala.

A Millennium of Weaving in Chiapas
Walter Morris, Jr.

Threading the light and dark colors in blocks creates more variety in the fabric. Here, the pattern switches every eight threads in the warp and the weft. Woven by the author, cotton warp and weft.

Variations in the Warp

Students can use the same method of changing the stripe direction in the weft to vary the pattern in the warp. They might use a light and dark sequence for 8 or 10 threads, and then switch that order by repeating two of the same color, as in the weft. This can create a wonderful variety of horizontal and vertical stripes when combined with the weft.

Have students determine the pattern they want in the warp, and then wind that sequence onto the loom. Or suggest that they switch the thread order in the very first row of weaving. Point out that, even if their warp is set up in a light and dark pattern across the width of the loom, they can switch a few selected threads and produce the same effect.

To achieve an even more complex pattern, students can have the stripes change direction in blocks. To do this, they must pick up two of the same warp colors next to each other on the shed stick. This will change the stripe the same way repeating a weft color did. Here, there are three light warps and then three dark warps on top of the shed stick.

Next, have students repeat the warp color sequence in the weft. Students can create all different kinds of log cabin block patterns once they have mastered this simple technique.

Finishing

Encourage students to continue weaving as far as possible. Then, have them cut the warp ends at the top, by the nails, and tie every two warps close to the last weft. Tell them to gently remove the other end of the fabric from the frame, and weave in any tails. The fabric will look much better if gently washed by hand, laid flat to dry, and pressed with an iron and a damp cloth.

Students can make a wide variety of fabrics on a frame loom. They can weave very quickly using a shed stick and heddle rod.

Music

Students can use the rhythm of a favorite song as inspiration for their stripe pattern. The width of each stripe reflects the long and short beat of the music. They can begin by clapping the beat, then writing down the pattern of short and long beats. These become thin and thick stripes.

Social Studies

In Scotland, after the wool was woven, it was finished by "waulking" the cloth. The length of fabric was soaked in warm water and then stomped on by the weaver and some friends. This was a social event with music providing a good strong beat as participants thumped the fabric under their bare feet. The resulting fabric was slightly felted, or fulled, allowing the fabric to be cut and sewn without unravelling.

Students can waulk cloth, using either their own weaving or commercial fabric. For the fulling action to be seen, you will need to use 100% wool. If you are using a commercial fabric, look for yardage that is loosely woven. You will observe about 10–25% shrinkage, depending on the length and vigor of the waulking. Be sure to measure the cloth before and after waulking so that students can figure the percentage of shrinkage in length and width. If you cannot locate traditional waulking songs to accompany your task, choose a folk song with a good dance beat.

The hair of sheep is called *fleece* while it is on the animal and after it is cut off or shorn. Once it is spun into yarn, it is called *wool.*

CHAPTER 4

Back Strap Looms

Ix Chebel Yak was the daughter of the Mayan moon goddess who taught the women of Guatemala, Honduras, and the Yucatan how to spin, dye, and weave.

The Book of Goddesses and Heroines
Patricia Monaghan

Back strap looms allow weavers to weave long warps without a large loom. One end of the warp on a back strap loom is tied around a fixed object, while the other is secured around the weaver's waist. As the weaver leans back, he or she produces tension to hold the warp in place. In many countries, back strap looms are used to create very complex fabrics. In the following lessons, students will explore some unique materials and weaving techniques using a rigid heddle device with a back strap loom.

Narrow bands of ikat threads are combined with thick and thin stripes of solid color in this fabric from Guatemala. This can be an economical use of dyed threads, as well as a dramatic pattern in the final fabric. Cotton warp and weft, from the collection of Ruth Beal.

Striped Belt

This back strap loom project creates a belt that is warp-faced. The pattern of the warp will dominate, creating a bold stripe pattern. Students will learn how to use a device called a **rigid heddle** to raise and lower the warp threads in an upper and lower shed on the loom. Once they are comfortable using a rigid heddle, they will be able to weave very quickly.

Vocabulary

rigid heddle, warp-faced, upper shed, lower shed, thrums, loom waste, back strap loom

Materials

See page 89 for instructions on building a rigid heddle.

Each student will need:

Masking tape

Scissors

Cardboard: small scraps for making stripe samples

Belt or wide ribbon to secure the warp around the waist

C-clamp or fixed object to secure the end of the warp (a post or tree)

Warp thread: several colors of a strong worsted weight yarn, about 32 yards

Weft thread: a thinner yarn that matches one of the warp colors, about 5 yards

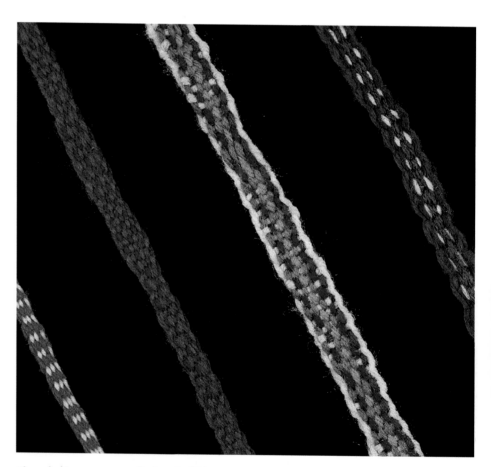

These belts were woven by fourth, fifth, and sixth graders on back strap looms made of craft sticks and tongue depressors. Students can vary the width of woven belts by changing the number of threads in the warp or by using thicker or thinner warp thread. Acrylic warp and weft.

Designing the Warp

The color combination of the warp threads is the major design element of this belt. Encourage students to take some time to experiment with the arrangement of the stripes. They should use no more than 16 warp threads. Invite students to try out their ideas by winding the colored yarn around small scraps of card-board or heavy paper. Have them try out symmetrical and asymmetrical arrangements of color and choose the one they like best.

To weave a belt 36" (91 cm) long, students need a 2-yard warp. The extra yarn in the warp is called **loom waste.** This is the yarn needed for the operation of the loom; it cannot be woven into the project. The yarn at the front that is tied around the weaver's belt, and the yarn at the back, is needed for the rigid heddle to move up and down. This loom waste is often used as fringe on the finished garment.

Preparing the Warp

Have students count the number of warp threads of each color they need and then cut the correct number of 2-yard lengths. Have them collect all the warp threads and tie them together with one large, loose overhand knot. Suggest that they comb out any tangled warp ends with their fingers. If their warp has fewer threads than the rigid heddle can accommodate, have them center the warp, leaving empty slots at each side.

The holes drilled in the wooden slats on the loom will each hold a single warp thread. This hole is called a

Once students even out the warp threads, have them tie all the threads together in an overhand knot.

In using a rigid heddle, students keep the same order of colors that they planned in the stripe. Each thread is either threaded through the small hole, or the space between the sticks.

heddle, and functions to raise or lower the thread placed through it. Every other thread in the warp will pass through one of the heddles. The remaining threads will be placed in the space between the wooden heddles.

Have students thread the first warp end through a heddle, then alternate threading the warp ends through a space or a heddle, keeping the color order that they planned for the finished belt. For example, if their pattern is: **4 blue, 2 red, 4 blue, 2 red, 4 blue,** they would first measure 12 blue warps, each 2 yards long, and 4 red warps, each 2 yards long. Then, they would knot them together, comb

out any tangles, and thread as follows:

blue in heddle,
blue in space,
blue in heddle,
blue in space,
red in heddle,
red in space,
blue in heddle,
blue in space,
blue in heddle,
blue in space,
red in heddle,
red in space,
blue in heddle,
blue in space,
blue in heddle,
blue in space.

If students are having trouble getting the yarn to go through the heddle, have them use a small piece of masking tape on the end to make a hard tip like a shoelace. This will thread easily through the hole.

Ask students to take a moment now to straighten out the warp. To do this, have them secure the far end on a C-clamp or around a post, pulling the warp threads so that they are evenly taut. Then, have them tie the warp threads together, keeping the tension even.

⧉ Weaving the Belt

Demonstrate the following steps for students, offering explanations and guidance as students weave their own belts.

1 Cut a 2-yard length of the weft yarn. Try to use the same color as the edge color of your warp. Using a thinner yarn for the weft allows the warp threads to dominate.

2 Tie one end of the warp to a secure object and the other end to your belt. Slide the rigid heddle close enough to allow you to reach it easily. Lean back to create tension on the warp, just enough to keep the warp threads firm.

Have students tie the knotted end of their warps to any stable anchor point. Weavers often use a tree or house post. In the classroom, several students can work on a C-clamp anchored to a corner of the desk or table.

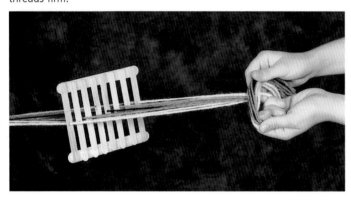

Keeping an even tension on all the threads, tie the end of the warp.

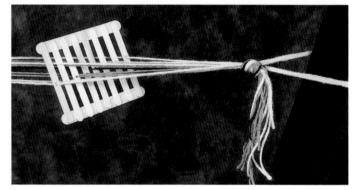

Belt loops, a belt, or any strong cord will anchor students into the other end of the loom.

3 Pull up on the heddle to raise every other thread in the warp. This is called the **upper shed**. Push down on the heddle to create the **lower shed**. You can weave plain weave by inserting the weft in the upper shed and, then, in the lower shed. Each time you change the shed, use the side of your hand to pack in the weft row you just inserted. This will produce a more even fabric.

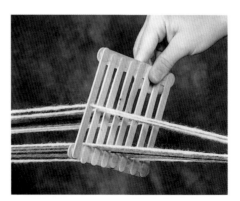

Demonstrate the upper shed on a back strap loom by pulling up on the rigid heddle. Explain that every other thread is held in the holes of the heddle.

Demonstrate the lower shed by pushing down on the rigid heddle. Explain that the threads that are in the holes of the heddle move down between the other threads.

4 To weave warp-faced fabric, be sure to pull the warp threads together—close enough so that they are touching—each time you weave a weft row. Pull the weft firmly to snug the warps together. This will bring out the stripe pattern. Because you are pulling the warps so close together, you do not have to worry about draw-in. The warp will be spread out through the rigid heddle, but will be narrow on the finished weaving. This is correct, not an error in your weaving.

5 As you weave, the fabric will build up in front of you, making it harder to reach the heddle. When this happens, stop and untie the warp from your belt. Now tie the woven fabric around your belt, bringing you closer to the heddle. You will need to do this several times before you finish the length of the belt.

6 If you run out of weft, leave the old weft hanging on one side and begin the new weft on the other side. After you are finished, use a tapestry needle to weave the tails into the fabric.

Each time students open a shed, remind them to use the side of their hand to clear any threads that might be sticking together. They can then bring the weft back through the shed as they remove their hand.

This band will be a warp-faced fabric if students are careful to pull the weft snugly each time they weave a weft row. The warp threads should be firmly packed next to each other. Students should barely see the weft thread.

Finishing

When students have finished weaving, have them untie both ends of the warp and remove the rigid heddle. If they wish to knot the fringe, they should do so before they trim it. After they have cut the fringe to the desired length, explain that the short lengths of yarn left over from the loom waste are called **thrums.**

Ix Chel was the Mayan snake-goddess of the moon, water, childbirth, and weaving. She was given shelter by the vulture god after being exiled from heaven by her jealous lover, the sun god. Mayan weavers today still weave stylized vultures and snakes into their huipils, or blouses.

The New Book of Goddesses and Heroines
Patricia Monaghan

Ikat Belt

Vocabulary

rigid heddle, warp-faced, upper shed, lower shed, ikat, loom waste, thrums

Materials

See page 89 for instructions on building a rigid heddle.

Each student will need:

Rigid heddle

Masking tape

Scissors

Belt or wide ribbon to secure the warp around the waist

C-clamp or fixed object to secure the end of the warp (a post or tree)

Dye: one color (Check the instructions to be sure it will dye your warp yarn.)

Rubber bands

Rubber gloves

Plastic garbage sacks, cut into 1" (3 cm) strips

Yarn for warp: a medium weight cotton or wool, about 32 yards. It is very important that the warp yarn not be synthetic because of the difficulty in dyeing synthetic yarns.

Yarn for weft: thinner than warp yarn, matching the warp color, about 5 yards

When warp threads are tie-dyed before they are woven, the pattern they produce is called **ikat**. This pattern will be most noticeable on warp-faced fabrics. The word ikat (pronounced *ee•cat*) means "to bind." Fabrics with tie-dyed warp threads are woven in many parts of the world, most notably in Malaysia, Japan, and Central America.

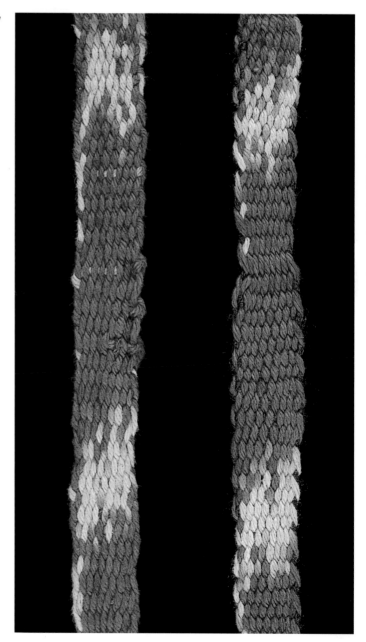

In this belt, woven by a fourth grade student, you can see the typical shimmering change of color on the ikat warp threads. Cotton ikat warp, cotton and acrylic weft.

Measuring, Tying, and Dyeing the Warp

Help students prepare the warp by following these steps.

1 Measure 16 warp threads, each 2 yards long. Tie a rubber band tightly around each end, securing the length of warp. Fold this length in half, and then in half again.

2 With the plastic strips, tie 1–2" (3–5 cm) segments as tightly as possible. These are the areas that will resist the dye. If they are loosely tied, the dye will penetrate and no pattern will show. The more ties you have, the more of the original color will remain after the dye bath.

Folding the warp threads in half length-wise, then in half again, before adding the plastic ties will produce a repeating pattern after the warp is dyed and the ties are removed. Here, you see the warp with plastic ties on it (top), the warp after it has been dyed (middle), and the warp threads with the plastic ties removed (bottom).

3 Dye the warp according to the directions on the dye package. Be sure to work in a ventilated area and wear rubber gloves when handling the dye or the dye-saturated warps. Cover counter space and do not work with dye in food preparation areas. Never allow students to work with dyes without adult supervision.

4 Rinse the dyed warp until the water runs clear and hang it to dry. Cut the ties off when the warp is dry, being careful not to cut the warp threads.

This ikat design is one that is woven by a girl of the Iban tribe on the island of Borneo when she reaches puberty. The weaving proves she is ready for marriage. Most Iban girls are married by the age of 13 or 14. Cotton warp and weft, from the collection of Lars Neises.

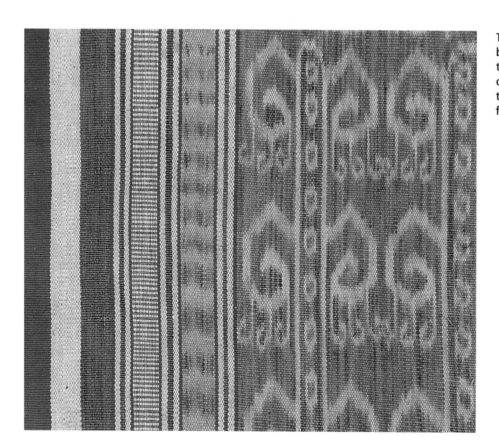

The ikat design in this detail of a *pua,* or blanket, from the Iban of Borneo is called the *mata hantu* or "spirit eyes." The border of the pua has solid color threads, framing the ikat design. Cotton warp and weft, from the collection of Lars Neises.

Threading the Rigid Heddle

When the dyed warps are dry, guide students through the following steps.

1 Remove the rubber band from one end of the warp. Comb out any tangled warp ends with your fingers. If there are fewer warp threads than the maximum number the rigid heddle will allow, center the threads by leaving empty heddles on either side.

2 Thread the first warp end through a space or a heddle. Alternate threading the warp ends through a space or a heddle. It doesn't matter whether you begin in a space or a heddle, as long as you keep the pattern. To make it easier to get the yarn through the heddle, use a small piece of masking tape on the end to make a hard tip like a shoelace.

3 Take a moment to straighten out the warp. Secure the far end on a C-clamp or around a post. Pull the warp threads so that they are evenly taut. Tie them together, keeping the tension even.

The pattern will show up best if the warp threads are packed tightly together. Using a thinner weft thread will also make the pattern in the warp show up more.

Weaving and Finishing the Belt

Students are now ready to strap themselves into their back strap looms. Review the weaving process described in the striped belt project with students. Offer individual help as needed.

Remind students to untie both ends of the warp when they have finished weaving. If they wish to knot the fringe, have them do it before they trim it to the desired length.

Several different ikat-patterned warp groups are mixed with a few solid-color warp stripes to produce this beautiful, shimmering fabric. Detail of a Guatemala ikat fabric, cotton warp and weft, collection of the author.

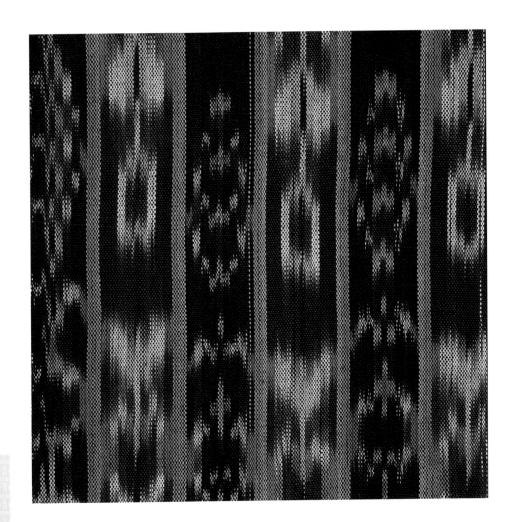

Weft Pictures

In Japan, kasuri fabric is woven of silk and the warp threads tied in ikat patterns. These master dyers have perfected a method for dying intricate pictures in both the warp and weft threads. As the weft is woven, the white pictures appear on the indigo-dyed cloth.

Japanese Ikat Weaving
Jun and Noriko Tomita

Nature Weaving

Vocabulary
rigid heddle, weft-faced, upper shed, lower shed

Materials
See page 89 for instructions on building a rigid heddle.

Each student will need:
Rigid heddle

Belt or wide ribbon to secure the warp around waist

C-clamp or fixed object to secure end of warp (a post or tree)

Masking tape

Scissors

Sticks or dowels: one or two, 6" (15 cm) long

Warp: a strong, thin thread in a neutral color, 32 total yards

Weft: a variety of materials gathered from nature; twigs, grasses, feathers, shells, etc.

Students will now use a back strap rigid heddle loom to create a wall hanging with natural elements. In the last two back strap lessons, students created warp-faced fabrics. For the wall hanging, they will be going back to weft-faced weaving using natural weft materials on a very widely spaced, thin warp.

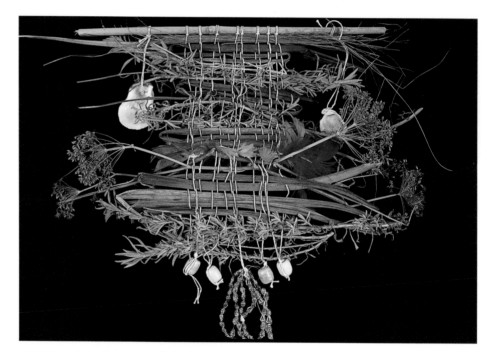

A sixth grade student created this hanging using a back strap loom and a variety of natural materials. Have students assemble their materials before they begin to weave. Once they are tied onto the warp threads, it will be difficult for them to move around. After they have finished their weavings, suggest that they add other objects to embellish their hangings. Cotton warp, natural materials, approximately 10 x 14" (25 x 36 cm).

Threading the Rigid Heddle

Demonstrate the following steps, and guide students as they thread their rigid heddles.

1 Measure 8 four-yard lengths of warp thread. Fold each warp thread in half.

2 Attach each warp to your 6" (15 cm) dowel with a lark's head knot (see below). Space out the knots so they are even with the spaces in the heddles of your loom. Comb out any tangled warp ends with your fingers. To thread the rigid heddle, work from the opposite end from the dowel.

A lark's head knot is a neat and efficient way to attach the warp. Space the knots out evenly along the dowel. The warp should be as wide as the loom.

3 Thread the first warp end through a space or a heddle. Alternate threading the warp ends through a space or a heddle.

4 Take a moment to straighten out the warp. Secure the dowel to a tabletop with a couple of pieces of tape. Pull on the warp threads as you even out the tension. When

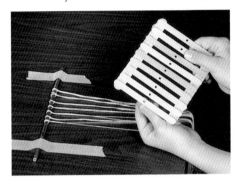

Taping the dowel to a flat surface will help students thread the warp in the same order they tied it to the dowel.

your warp is straight and even, tie a knot in the end.

5 Secure the knotted end on a C-clamp or around a post. Tie the ends of the dowel to the belt or ribbon that is around your waist. Be sure that your materials for weft are close by before you tie yourself into the loom.

With the dowel at one end of the warp, it is easy for students to tie themselves into the back strap loom.

Weaving and Finishing

Review with students how to begin weaving on their back strap looms. Remind them, as they insert the weft in the upper shed and, then, in the lower shed, to place each weft row close to the last row. Some of their weft rows may be irregular or fragile, so it will be hard to pack them as tightly as they have in other projects. However, with the thin warp threads spread apart, the weft will show.

Suggest that students might want to weave some areas back and forth, selvage to selvage. Or, they might consider leaving wefts that stick out from the selvage, creating texture. If students want to add objects to their weavings, such as shells or beads, simply drill a hole in any object that

needs one and string them on a one-yard piece of yarn. Then, have students weave in this new weft, making sure to pull the object to the front of the weaving as they work. When hangings are as long as desired, students can weave in another dowel or stick to use as the bottom of the piece.

When they have finished weaving, have students untie the far end of the warp from the C-clamp. Have them cut or untie the knot at this end and slide the rigid heddle off the warp. Then, instruct them to knot the ends of the warp close to the last row of weft. They may add beads or shells to the fringe.

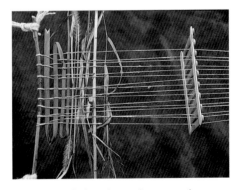

This is a weft-faced weaving, so make sure students pack their weft in tightly to dominate the widely spaced, thin warp threads. Students might want to have some of the weft elements protrude to either side of the weaving.

Nature Weaving • 65

Science

If students use cotton or wool yarn for the ikat belt, they can gather natural materials to create their own dyes. Collect onion skins, walnut shells, turmeric spice, marigold flowers, or tree leaves, such as poplar, willow, or peach, for making the dye. A chemical called a mordant is needed to encourage the fiber molecules to bind with the dye. A common and safe source is alum from the grocery store. If students want to experiment with copper mordants, they can add pennies to the dye bath.

After they have measured and tied their warp threads, prepare the dye bath by simmering the dye material in water for at least one hour. Strain the liquid and simmer the warp chains in the dye and mordant for one hour. If you are using wool yarn, add a bit of vinegar to the dye and mordant solution to create an acid bath. With wool, it is possible to felt the fiber by too much agitation while the yarn is hot. Allow the threads to cool completely before removing them from the dye bath, and rinse thoroughly.

Countries that produce ikat fabrics include Guatemala, Peru, Ecuador, Colombia, Mexico, the Ivory Coast, Nigeria, Ghana, Afghanistan, India, the Philippines, Japan, Thailand, Cambodia, and Indonesia.

Japanese Ikat Weaving
Jun and Noriko Tomita

These stylised animals are some of the many patterns created by complex ikat dyeing in Sumbawa, east of Bali. Cotton warp and weft, from the collection of Lars Neises.

CHAPTER 5

Beads, Braids, and Baskets

Beading, braiding, and basketry are crafts related to the art of weaving. These crafts are made with special types of looms that are easily made and used by students. The following lessons do not necessarily require any previous weaving experience.

The Athapascan people in western Canada used a bow loom to create quilled bands. The warp thread was stretched between the two ends of a stick or branch. This held the threads taut, like the string of a bow. Instead of beads, small dyed pieces of bird quills or porcupine quills were threaded onto the loom. Very intricate designs were woven of colored quills.

Weaving Arts of the North American Indian
Frederick J. Dockstader

Even young students can make wonderful, functional baskets.

Bead Looms

Beads are most often strung into necklaces, bracelets, and anklets. They are sewn onto clothing, dolls, or masks. In North America, native artists use a simple loom to weave glass beads into bands. The bands can then be sewn onto leather or cloth. Although the bands are strong, the beads appear to float unsupported. Students will enjoy using a bead loom to weave beaded straps for jewelry or bags.

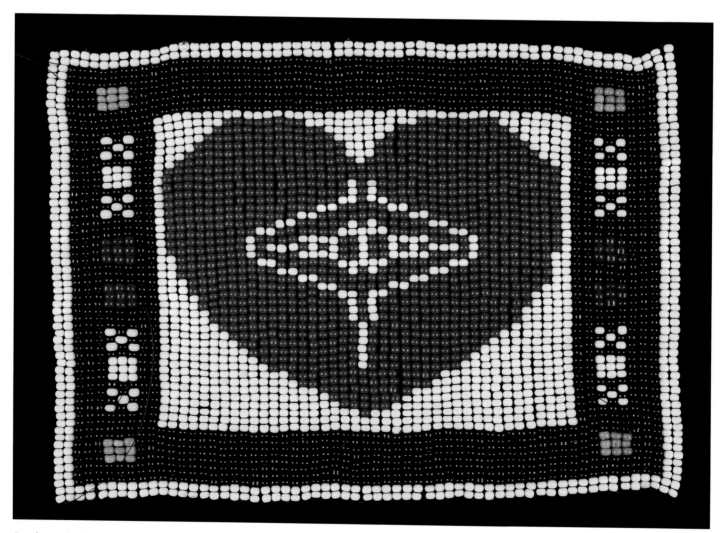

**Bead weaving by Rebecca Laurence, 1997.
Seed beads, 2½ x 4" (6 x 10 cm). Courtesy
of the artist.**

Woven Seed Bead Bracelet

Vocabulary
seed beads

Materials
See page 90 for instructions on building a bead loom.

Each student will need:

Bead loom

#8 seed beads: at least 2 colors

Beading thread for warp and weft
  (i.e., Nymo "D" thread)

Beading needle: #10 sharp

Graph paper

Colored pencils

Pin cushion

Lid from plastic container to hold
  beads

In the old days, when people hung a beaded strip from the pyramid poles of the tipi, you knew a young girl lived there. If there was fourteen hooves decorated with corn, a young teenage boy lived in the tipi.

Cheyenne beadworker,
Mary Armstrong
(from *Piecework*,
July/August 1998)

Most students love designing beautiful patterns to weave into jewelry. This project uses small, round, glass beads, called **seed beads,** in a bracelet design. Seed beads are made by cutting a tube of colored glass into small pieces and then polishing them down into smooth beads about the size of seeds.

Students can weave any design that they can graph out on paper, including geometric designs, and letters. A variety of bead-woven bracelets by fifth and sixth graders, #8 seed beads, each bracelet approximately ½ x 7" (1 x 18 cm).

⊞ Warping the Bead Loom

Demonstrate the following steps for students, then monitor their work.

1 Tie the beading thread onto the screw at one end of the loom. Use several knots to hold the thread tightly. Leave a tail about 6" (15 cm) long.

Be sure students tie the beading thread securely. It will need to stay taut while they are weaving. Have them leave a long tail so that they can tie off the last thread.

3 Wind the thread around the screw twice and then tie it to the tail you left at the start.

Several knots will hold the warp threads securely on the loom. Using an even number of warp threads will allow students to tie the last warp to the tail they left on the first warp.

2 Stretch the thread to the other end of the loom, loop it around the screw, and return to where you began. Loop the thread around this screw, and repeat until you have six warp threads.

Have students stretch the thread tightly as they warp the loom, but do not worry about uneven spacing. After they have the first row of beads on the loom, the spacing will even out.

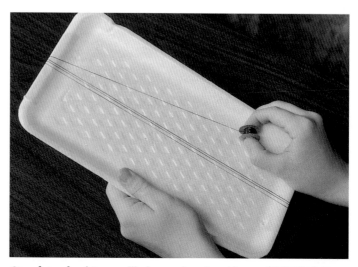

Styrofoam food trays will also work as bead looms. WARNING: **Do not use food trays that have been in contact with raw meat. Use only new trays or trays used for non-meat items.** Reinforce the top and bottom edge with tape to keep the beading thread from cutting through the Styrofoam. Tape the first and last warp threads to the back of the tray. Wind the warp threads around the tray, keeping a tight tension on them.

Designing a Pattern

Have students choose colored pencils that match the bead colors they wish to use in their bracelets. Two or three colors will be enough to make an interesting design.

Show students that the horizontal rows on graph paper relate to the rows of beads on the loom. The vertical lines, or columns, on the graph paper relate to the warp threads on the loom. For this project, students will be working with six warps.

Explain that they will always have one more warp thread than they have beads in each row. This means that, for this project, students will design a pattern for five beads in each row. You might write an equation on the chalkboard to help students remember this ratio:

warps = beads per row + 1

Have students color the squares on the graph paper to match the pattern they wish to weave.

Students can create a wide range of designs with bead weaving. Be sure to have a system for managing the seed beads and beading needles, as they are very small and easy to lose. Good lighting is also important for this detailed work.

Weaving the Bracelet and Taking It off the Loom

Explain the following steps as you demonstrate for students.

1 Thread the needle with a yard of beading thread. Overlap the end of the thread slightly, but do not double the thread or knot it at the end. Work with a single strand of beading thread.

Have students cut a weft thread about one yard long and tie one end to the first warp thread. This knot will slide up and down on the warp until students have a few rows of beading done. They should slide the knot a few inches from the end of the loom, to allow room to tie off the warp threads when they are finished weaving.

2 Tie the end of the thread to the farthest left warp. Place the knot several inches from the end of the loom. Leave at least 6" (15 cm) of warp thread on each end of the finished bracelet to tie off for fringe.

3 Pick up the beads that match the first row on your graph paper design. Be sure they are in the same order on your needle as on

Keep seed beads in plastic lids. A single layer of beads will allow students to see all the colors and to pick up one bead at a time with the tip of the needle.

the graph sheet. Slide the beads over the needle and down the thread.

4 Bring the needle, beads, and thread UNDER the warps and position the beads so that there is one warp thread between each bead.

Once the beads are on the needle, students slide them onto the thread. Then, they pass the needle and thread under the warp threads.

CONTINUED ON FOLLOWING PAGE

5 Push the beads up from below with your index finger until the beads pop up through the warps. Each warp should have only one bead between it and the next warp. Press the beads up firmly from below while you pass the needle back to the left, going THROUGH the hole in each bead. Be sure that the weft thread is on top of the warp threads on this second pass through the beads. This will secure the first row of beads.

6 You are now ready to pick up the beads in the next row of your design. Continue to weave each row, referring to your graph paper to establish the pattern.

The first row of beads will be the hardest to position. Students need to get one bead between each warp thread. When the beads are in position, they press them up firmly with one finger. The holes of the beads should be above the warps.

Now students can easily pass the needle back through the beads. On this trip, the needle and the weft thread should be above the warps. The more firmly students press up on the beads, the easier it is to keep the weft above the warp.

Have students continue to repeat these steps, using their graph paper plans to tell them which beads are next.

7 When there is only 8–10" (20–25 cm) of beading thread left on the needle, it is time to splice in a new piece. Secure the old thread by weaving it through the last 5–6 rows of beads. For instance, if you are on row 20 of your pattern and are low on thread, stop adding beads and go back through the beads in rows 19, 18, 17, 16, and 15. Cut off any extra thread. Then, measure out another yard of weft, thread the needle, and start back on row 15. Pass the needle and thread through rows 15–20 and pick up on your design where you left off.

8 When you are finished beading your pattern, secure the last row of beads in the same way as the splice, weaving your thread back through the last 5–6 rows of beading.

9 Cut the threads by the screws on each end. Once the bands are off the looms tie the warp fringe in one overhand knot as close to the beads as possible. Thread a clasp on each end or slide larger beads onto the fringe.

As the beads seem to float between the warp threads, it is easy for students to see how geometric shapes can be created with the beads.

If warp threads are too loose, show students how to take up some of the slack by inserting a pencil or marker at one or both ends of the loom.

Beaded Medicine Pouch

Once students have woven a narrow band, encourage them to try something larger. Point out that a wider design allows lots of options for patterns.

Vocabulary
seed beads

Materials
See page 90 for instructions on building a bead loom.

Each student will need:

Bead loom

#8 seed beads: at least 2 colors

Beading thread for warp and weft
  (i.e., Nymo size "D" or "A")

Beading needle: #10

Graph paper

Colored pencils

Pin cushion

Lid from plastic container to hold
  beads

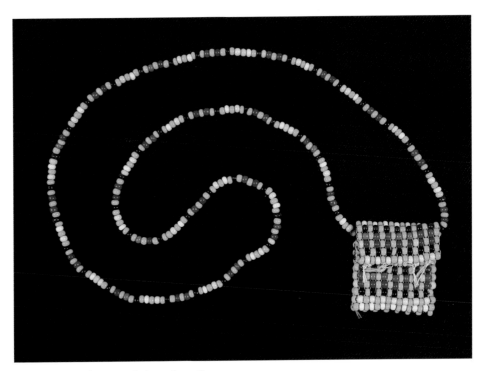

Once students have made bracelets, they can create larger items with bead weaving. This medicine bag was woven by a sixth grader with #8 seed beads.

Stampede by Sharon Bateman. Bead weaving of a wildebeest stampede. Seed beads, 3 x 5" (8 x 13 cm), collection of Judith Gilmartin.

⊞ Warping the Bead Loom and Designing a Pattern

See the beaded bracelet lesson for complete directions on threading the loom. Thread the loom with 16 warp threads for this medicine bag.

Have students choose the colored pencils that match the bead colors they wish to use in their bag designs. Review the relationship between the graph paper design and the weaving on the loom. For this project, students will be working with 16 warps. Remind them that they will always have one more warp thread than beads in each row. Refer back to the equation: **warps = beads per row + 1.** So, for this project, students will design a pattern for 15 beads in each row.

Direct students to plan to weave a piece about 3" (8 cm) long. Have them color the squares on the graph paper in the pattern they wish to weave. Point out that the larger number of beads in their patterns allows more design options.

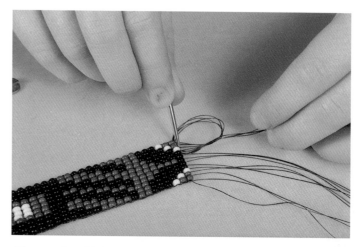

When students' bags are approximately 3" (8 cm) long, they can cut the warps and tie them off in small groups of 2–4 threads.

Weaving and Taking the Bag off the Loom

Refer back to the beaded bracelet lesson for details on the bead weaving technique. Provide students with long beading needles for this wider project.

Have students cut the threads off by the screws on each end. Have them tie the warp threads together in small groups close to the last row of beads on each end. Once off the loom, students can transform the flat beadwork into a pouch by overlapping the lower 1¼" (3 cm). Direct them to stitch both sides together with the beading thread, pointing out that the ½" (1 cm) remaining will create a flap.

Students can use the warp threads to add a beaded fringe at either end of the bag. For a beaded strap on the bag, they should measure out a thread twice the length needed, and thread their needle. Have them tie the end securely onto one edge of the bag and string beads for the neckpiece. Make sure their thread is doubled for this part of the project. They can tie off the other end when it is beaded to the correct length.

Have students sew the sides of the bead weaving together to create a pouch.

Diptych with Cat by Rebecca Laurence, 1997. Seed beads, 4 x 6" (10 x 15 cm), courtesy of the artist.

Kumihimo Braids

Kumihimo is a Japanese technique for making a complex multi-strand braid. The ornate band is very strong, and is traditionally used in Japan to tie together the samurai warrior's armor. Today, it is a decorative accessory to the Japanese kimono. A kumihimo, or *obijime*, is tied around the outside of an *obi* — a wide sash worn around the waist.

Traditional kumihimo looms are wooden disks with a hole in the center. The disk is mounted on a stand and fibers are braided by moving bobbins around the disk. The braid grows in the center of the disk, dropping down underneath as it is completed. Because this is a braiding technique rather than weaving, there is only one set of threads instead of a warp and a weft.

Once students learn how to make an eight-strand spiral braid, they can experiment with more colors and different arrangement of threads. These braids were all made on a simple cardboard loom, each using sixteen threads. Kumihimo braids by Jean Parodi.

Braided Bracelet

Materials

See page 91 for instructions on building a kumihimo loom.

Each student will need:

Kumihimo loom

Tapestry needle: large-eyed

Scissors

Yarn: preferably worsted weight,
  2 colors of 4 strands each, 8
  1-yard lengths

These braids are fast and fun to make. Students can explore different color combinations with the simple eight-strand spiral braid. Once they have mastered the basic technique for creating the cord, they can experiment with different colors and more threads to create their own patterns.

Students can use any number of colors for a kumihimo braid. However, it is easiest to learn the basic pattern with only two colors. Starting out with an eight-strand braid will make getting started fun and easy.

Sixth grade students wove these kumihimo cords with acrylic yarn.

Setting Up the Loom

Have students tie all eight strands together in an overhand knot, then slip this knot through the hole in the center of the loom. Instruct students to divide the strands into pairs, two threads of the same color, then place one pair in two slots at the north position on the loom, and the other pair of that color in the south position. Direct students to place the other color pairs in the east and west positions.

Have students begin with all the threads together in the center of the loom. Then, have them spread the threads around the circle.

Weaving the Braid

Demonstrate these steps for students. Explain that the strands will be changing places around the loom, creating an interlacement at the center.

1 Hold the loom with one hand and bring the bottom left thread up, placing it to the left of the two strands in the north. There are now three strands at the top and one at the bottom.

2 Move the thread on the right top to the bottom right. All the strands are now in pairs again, but they have shifted slightly.

3 Rotate the loom clockwise until the strands that were in the east and west positions are now in the north and south positions. Continue moving the strands from the bottom left to the top left, and the top right to the bottom right. Then rotate clockwise.

When students are moving the threads on the left, they hold the loom in their right hand. When they switch to move the right side threads, they hold the loom in their left hand.

Show students how to give a pull on the cord as it emerges under the loom to even out the braid.

1 Place **A** threads (shown in red) in the north and south position. Place **B** threads (shown in blue) in the east and west position.

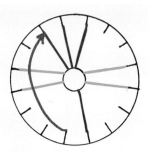

2 Move the lower left **A** thread to the upper left.

3 Move the upper right **A** thread to the notch to the right of the lower **A** thread. Now there are again two threads in the north and south position.

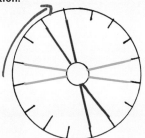

4 Rotate the disc a quarter turn clockwise.

5 The **B** threads are now in the north and south position.

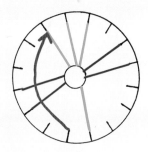

6 Repeat steps 1–3 with the **B** threads.

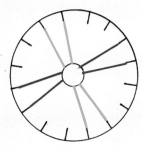

7 Each time the threads will return to this positon.

As students weave, direct them to pull the lengthening braid gently through the center. If they leave the weaving and come back to it later, have them look at the threads in the center to see which set is on top of the other strands. That will be the set that was moved last. Tell them to rotate the loom and resume the pattern.

If the unbraided threads get tangled on the sides of the loom, have students pull the threads out one at a time. Combing through them will result in a knot. If students pull them out singly, the threads will straighten out easily.

To change the direction of the spiral, have students move the bottom right thread up and the top left thread down.

Finishing

When their braids measure 7" (18 cm), have students remove the strands from the loom and untie the knot at the start of the braid. Have them cut the fringe to 1" (3 cm) long. Show them how to overlap the fringes, wrap a strand of yarn tightly around them, and bind them together, sealing the cut ends inside. Use a tapestry needle to pull the two ends inside the wrapping. Trim off any excess threads.

Basket Weaving

Baskets are often woven in a plain weave structure out of all kinds of natural materials. Students can create baskets using the same plain weave pattern that they used to make fabric. Basketry is too complex a process to be done by machine. All baskets are woven by hand. You might take this opportunity to impress upon students the value of craftwork and the importance of good craftsmanship.

Traditional rush basket from Peru, woven rush and grasses, 14 x 4 x 10" (36 x 10 x 25 cm), from the collection of Jane Schelly.

Woven Basket

Materials

Each student will need:

Glue stick

Scissors

Ruler

Pencil

Construction paper: 1 strip of 1 x 18" (3 x 46 cm) in a color to match the yarn

Yarn: worsted weight, a variety of colors, about 10 yards total

Tag board or index paper: 2 pieces, 4 x 8" (10 x 20 cm) and 3 x 9" (8 x 23 cm)

Here is a chance for students to use their weaving skills to make baskets. Baskets are woven around in a circle, similar to the pouch made on the cardboard loom. This basket can be made in different sizes. The directions given here will make a basket about 3 x 4" (8 x 10 cm).

Fifth graders created these woven baskets using yarn, construction paper, and tag board. The finished baskets are not only beautiful, but very sturdy and functional. The round basket was made using a paper plate as a base.

⊞ Making the Bottom and Spokes

As you demonstrate the following steps, have students follow along.

1 Draw a line 2½" (6 cm) from the short end of each piece of tag board.

2 Glue the two pieces together at a right angle, matching the lines to center the pieces.

3 Fold each of the flaps in, overlapping the center rectangle. Now, unfold the flaps.

4 With a ruler, or by estimating, divide both 3" (8 cm) wide flaps and one 4" (10 cm) wide flap into an even number of strips. This could be 4 or 6, but it is important that it be an even number.

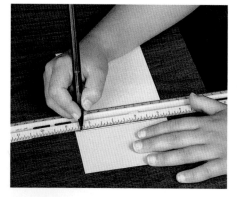

Have students mark a line 2½" (6 cm) from the edge of both cards. This will help them to center one card over the other.

When one card is lined up over the other, have students glue the two together.

Have students fold all four flaps over the center section.

5 Divide the last flap into an odd number of strips. These will be the spokes of the basket. It is important to have an odd number of spokes in order to weave plain weave around in a circle.

6 Cut each spoke from the edge of the flap to the edge of the center rectangle. Do not cut the bottom of the basket.

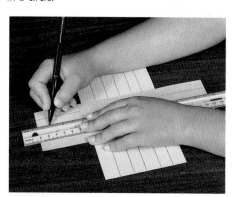

One flap must have an odd number of strips, and the rest even numbers.

Have students cut the flaps to where the cards intersect.

⊞ Weaving the Basket

Demonstrate these steps and have students follow along.

1 Begin anywhere, weaving a strand of yarn over and under the spokes. Once you have gone completely around the basket, you should be weaving the opposite pattern from the first row. Take a moment to tighten the yarn enough to make the spokes stand up straight.

Check that students weave the first row around the strips in an over and under pattern.

2 Weave around the entire basket a second time. Adjust the tension on the yarn so all that the spokes are upright, none of them leaning into or out of the basket.

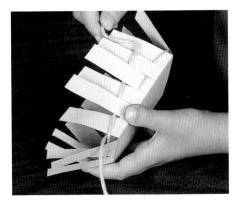

When students get back to where they started weaving, their second row should automatically be opposite from the first row. If they have the same pattern weaving in their second row, check to make sure they have an odd number of strips. If this is not the problem, double check their first pattern row.

3 Continue weaving around the basket until you wish to change colors. Leave a 3" (8 cm) tail of yarn hanging on the outside of the basket. Lay the new color in the same pattern as the old color, overlapping the yarns for 4 or 5 spokes. Continue weaving around the basket with the new color.

Show students how to change wefts by overlapping the yarn for a few inches. This will produce an area with a doubled weft. Pack down the weft so it no longer shows.

4 Make sure to pack down the yarn as you weave around the basket. The yarn should cover the tag board spokes completely.

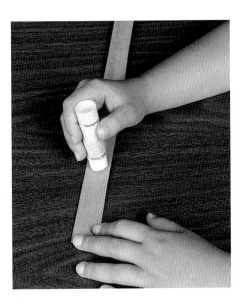

When students have woven to within ½" (1 cm) of the top of the basket, ask them to check if they can pack the wefts in any more. If not, they are ready to add the reinforcing strip at the top. Have them fold the long paper strip in half lengthwise, and add glue.

▦ Finishing

Instruct students to stop weaving when they are ½" (1 cm) from the top of the spokes. Have them fold the long strip of construction paper in half lengthwise, put glue along the entire length of the paper, and place it carefully around the top edge of the spokes. Tell students to overlap the construction paper so that there is no gap in the top edge of the basket. Students can now trim off any tails on the outside of the basket even with the surface.

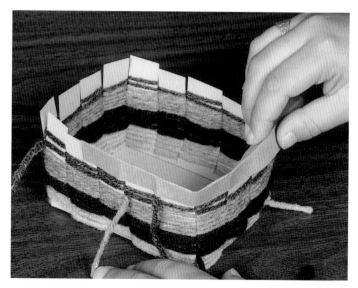

Demonstrate how to sandwich the cardboard strips of the basket in the paper strip. Work your way around the basket, overlapping where you started.

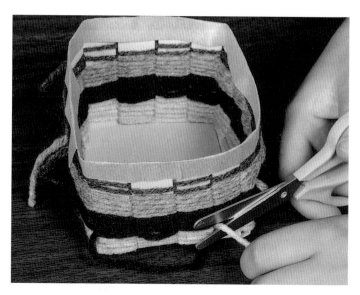

Students should trim off any yarn tails flush with the surface of the basket.

What is my goddess making?

Saule is plaiting a sieve, a basket

in which to sift the spring rain.

Look! Her little daughter is dressed

in a garment of dew. Her fair hair

is hidden beneath a white veil

and over the veil is a wreath

her mother wove of fresh leaves

Lithuanian folksong,
The Goddess Path,
Patricia Monaghan

Math

Once they have designed their bead pattern on paper, have students determine how many beads of each color they will need. They can count each color and multiply by the number of times the design is repeated. Or, they can count the number of beads in each row and multiply by the number of rows in the pattern to find the total number of beads, then estimate the percentage of each color. Once the bracelet is woven they can check their estimate with the final product.

Movement

Students who are kinesthetic learners can act out the braiding process. Have eight students be the thread. Standing in a circle, they move in the braiding sequence, switching places and all rotating around the circle.

Creative Writing/Social Studies

Have students brainstorm ideas and then write about what their baskets might have been used for in another time. Have students imagine themselves as basket makers in another time and place, and then discuss how the basket would look and what would be stored in it.

> Kumihimo means 'the gathering of threads,' and it is a general word applied to braiding.
>
> *Braids*
> Rodrick Owen

Students will love making spiral braids. Very simple materials are needed, and the technique is so easy to learn. Invite students to think of creative uses for their braids.

Building Looms

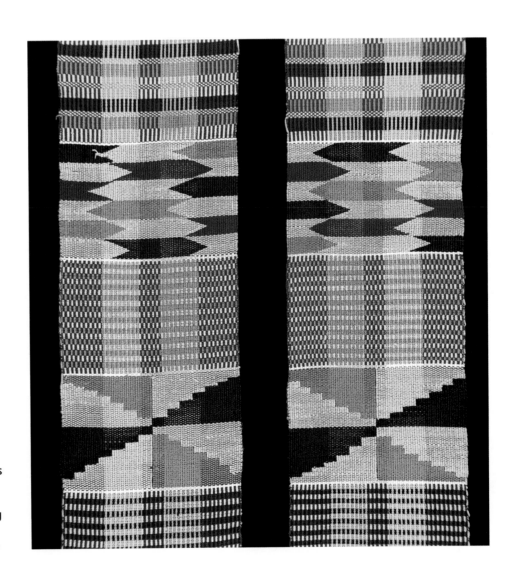

Kente cloth from Ghana. This fabric is woven by men on narrow looms. The tension on the warp is created by placing a drag weight on the threads, which are stretched out a distance from the loom. As the fabric is woven, the weighted warp is pulled closer. This is the reverse of the process that many cultures use in weaving on back strap looms. Cotton warp and weft. From the collection of Sharon Hinze.

Frame Loom

1 Build or purchase a wooden frame about 8 x 10" (20 x 25 cm). Art supply stores carry stretcher bars in many sizes. These frames have corners that slide into each other with no tools needed.

2 Draw a line on each end ½" (1 cm) from the inside edge of the frame.

3 Mark the spacing for the nails by making a dot on the line every ¼" (½ cm).

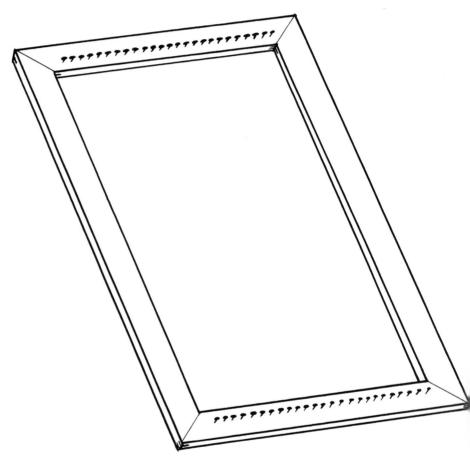

Wood stretcher bars, about 8 x 10"

Space nails every ¼". Leave ¼–½" of the nail heads showing. Be sure top and bottom nails line up with each other.

Rigid Heddle

1 Gather two tongue depressors and nine craft sticks for each loom.

2 Mark a dot in the center of each craft stick. It is important that these dots line up on all the craft sticks.

3 Drill a ⅛" (.3 cm) hole in each craft stick on the center dot.

4 Lay the two tongue depressors parallel to each other at a distance equal to the width of the craft sticks. Lay the craft sticks evenly across the tongue depressors. Space them evenly, and glue the ends onto the tongue depressors with wood glue or other strong white glue.

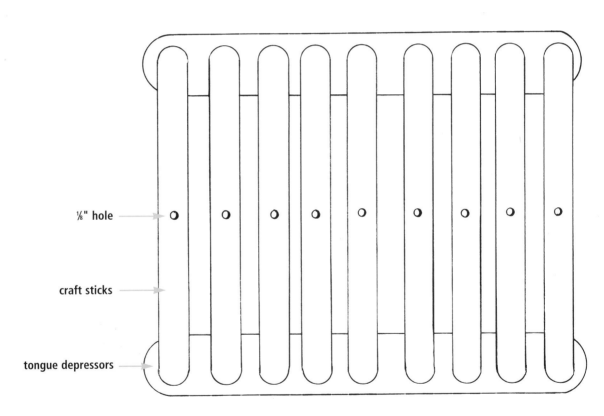

⅛" hole

craft sticks

tongue depressors

Glue craft sticks to tongue depressors after holes are drilled.

Bead Loom

1 Attach four metal corner braces to the sides of a scrap of wood about 1 x 4 x 12" (3 x 10 x 30 cm) using wood screws. (If the wood splits, drill the holes.)

2 Put a screw into the center of each end of the board, only partially tightening the screws down. These screws need to protrude to anchor the threads on the loom.

3 Thread 4" (10 cm) machine screws through the holes in the corner braces, adding nuts on both inside corners. Thread wing nuts on each end.

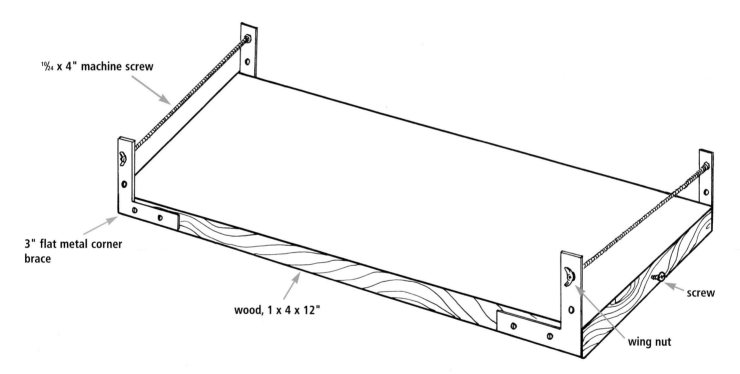

$^{10}\!/_{24}$ **x 4" machine screw**

3" flat metal corner brace

wood, 1 x 4 x 12"

screw

wing nut

Looms can vary in size.

Kumihimo Loom

1 Cut a 5" (13 cm) square out of light-weight cardboard.

2 These looms can be either round or octagonal. For both shapes, use a ruler to draw lines from corner to corner on the square. Then, draw a line down the center of the square and another across the center of the square. All the lines should intersect at a center point.

3 From the center point, measure and mark 2½" (6 cm) towards each of the four corners. For the circle loom, draw a circle that intersects these marks. Cut out the circle. For the octagonal loom, cut off the four corners using the marks as a guide.

4 Make 16 notches equally spaced around the edge of the cardboard shape.

5 With a pushpin, make a small hole in the center of the cardboard shape. Enlarge the hole with a pencil, twisting the pencil until it fits easily through the hole. (Adults can use a craft knife to cut a ½" (1 cm) hole in the center of the cardboard.)

Looms can be larger or smaller.

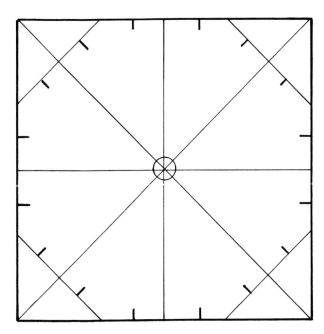

Divide square into eighths.
Cut corners off a 5" square of cardboard.
Cut ½" hole in center.
Cut ¼" notches on each side (16 total).

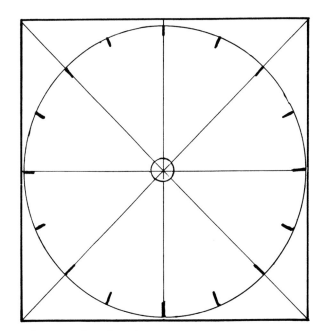

5" square of cardboard.
Cut ½" hole in center.
Cut 16 notches, ¼" deep around edge.

Glossary

Balanced plain weave A fabric in which there are the same number of warp threads per inch as weft threads; single weft threads weave an over one, under one pattern.

Basket weave A variation of plain weave in which the weft skips over two and under two warp threads.

Back strap A simple loom in which the weaver ties one end of the warp around the waist and the other around a fixed object. The weaver leans back to create tension on the warps.

Cartoon The drawing used to create a tapestry.

Clasped weft A simplified tapestry method in which two wefts share the same shed. Two different colors, one from the right and one from the left, meet in the center of the warp. The two colors are interlocked and exit the shed in the same direction they entered.

Color-weave effect When the colors of the warp and weft yarns interact with the weave structure to create a complex appearance.

Dovetailing A technique that interlocks areas of color in a weaving by having a weft thread of each color share one warp thread.

Draw-in A narrowing of the fabric during weaving, caused by not having enough weft. Draw-in can be avoided by leaving an arc in the weft with each row.

Heddle A device for holding a warp thread, raising or lowering it to form a shed. A heddle can be as simple as a loop of yarn or a hole drilled in a stick.

Heddle rod A dowel or stick used to hold a set of string heddles, allowing them to function as a unit, raising a set of warp threads.

Ikat A process of tie-dyeing warp threads before weaving that produces a color pattern in the warp.

Log cabin A variation of plain weave using a light and dark pattern in the warp and weft. The interaction of the colors in the threads forms horizontal and vertical stripes.

Loom waste Warp thread that is necessary to the functioning of the loom, such as the slack needed to open a shed or in tying knots at one or both ends, but not to the woven pattern.

Lower shed The triangular opening between the warp threads that is formed when a rigid heddle is pushed down on the warp threads.

Mock tapestry See *clasped weft*.

Plaid The color pattern formed in fabric when a stripe pattern in the warp is repeated in the weft.

Plain weave A weaving pattern produced when one weft is woven under one warp, then over one warp.

Pick and pick The technique of changing between two weft colors in each row of weaving. For instance, weaving a row of light weft, then dark, then light, then dark.

Pile weave A technique that produces a tufted effect on the surface of the fabric, mostly used for rugs.

Rigid heddle A frame that holds a set of heddles. The frame is then used to create sheds in the warp.

Rya A Scandinavian pile weave based on knots. The knots alternate with rows of plain weave to create a stable fabric.

Seed bead A very small, round, glass bead.

Selvage The finished edge on the right and left sides of fabric that is formed by the weft turning the corner and weaving back through the warp. (The other two sides of the rectangular fabric are called the *raw edges*.)

Shed The triangular opening between the warp threads that is produced when some warps are raised or lowered. The weft is passed through the shed in weaving.

Shed stick A smooth, flat stick that is used to raise warp threads, producing a shed.

Slit Weaving A technique that forms an opening, or slit, between areas of color in a weaving, producing sharp color changes and geometric shapes.

Tabby See *plain weave*.

Tapestry A weave structure characterized by discontinuous wefts in one row. The changing of weft colors in this manner allows pictures to be woven into the fabric.

Tartan A plaid fabric that is associated with a particular Scottish clan and is registered with the Scottish Tartan Society.

Thrums The loom waste that is cut off the finished project.

Twill A basic weave characterized by a diagonal line.

Upper shed The triangular opening between the warp threads formed when a rigid heddle is pulled up on the warp threads.

Vertical point twill A variation of twill weave that produces a zigzag pattern.

Warp The set of threads in woven fabric that are held under tension on a loom.

Warp-faced weave A fabric characterized by a dominance of warp threads. Use of a warp thicker than the weft will create a warp-faced weave, as will crowding the warp threads closely together.

Weave Interlacement of warp and weft.

Weft The set of threads that cross the warp at a right angle. The weft threads are woven over and under the warp threads.

Weft-faced weave A weave in which the warp threads are hidden by the weft threads. Use of a thin, widely spaced warp and a thick weft will produce a weft-faced weave.

Bibliography

Barber, Elizabeth Wayland. *Women's Work, The First 20,000 Years: Women, Cloth, and Society in Early Times.* New York: W. W. Norton, 1994.

*Bunch, Roger and Bunch, Roland. *The Highland Maya: Patterns of Life and Clothing in Guatemala.* Visalia: Indigenous Publications, 1977.

Crockett, Candace. *Card Weaving.* Loveland: Interweave Press, 1991.

*_____. *The Complete Spinning Book.* New York: Watson-Guptill, 1977.

*Dockstader, Frederick J. *Weaving Arts of the North American Indian.* New York: Thomas Crowell, 1978.

*Gordon, Beverly. *Feltmaking: Tradtions, Techniques, and Contemporary Explorations.* New York: Watson-Guptill, 1980.

Harris, Jennifer, ed. *Textiles 5,000 Years: An International History and Illustrated Survey.* New York: Harry N. Abrams, Inc., 1993.

Held, Shirley E. *Weaving, A Handbook of the Fiber Arts.* New York: Harcourt Brace Javonovich College and School Division, 1998.

*Hecht, Ann. *The Art of the Loom: Weaving, Spinning and Dyeing Across the World.* New York: Rizzoli, 1989.

Housego, Jenny. *Tribal Rugs: An Introduction to the Weaving of the Tribes of Iran.* New York: Interlink Pub Group, 1998.

Hull, Alastair and Barnard, Nicholas and Merrell, James. *Living with Kilims.* London: Thames and Hudson, 1995.

Jobes, Gertrude. *Dictionary of Mythology, Folklore, and Symbols.* Lanham, MD: Scarecrow Press, 1962.

Monaghan, Patricia. *The Goddess Path: Myths, Invocations & Rituals.* St. Paul: Llewellyn, 1999.

_____. *The New Book of Goddesses & Heroines.* St. Paul: Llewellyn, 1997.

*Morris, Walter. *A Millennium of Weaving in Chiapas: An Introduction to the Pellizzi Collection of Chiapas Textiles.* Chiapas: San Jolobil, 1984

*Morrison, Phylis. *Spiders' Games.* Seattle: University of Washington Press, 1979.

Owen, Rodrick. *Braids: 250 Patterns from Japan, Peru & Beyond.* Loveland: Interweave Press, 1995.

Schevill, Margot Blum. *Maya Textiles of Guatemala: The Gustavas A. Eisen Collection.* Austin: University of Texas Press, 1993.

*Tomita, Jun and Tomita, Noriko. *Japanese Ikat Weaving, The Techniques of Kasuri.* London: Routledge & Kegan Paul, 1982.

Urquhart, Blair, ed. *Tartans.* Secaucus: Chartwell, 1994

*Wilson, Jean. *Weaving is for Everyone.* New York: Van Nostrand Reinhold Company, 1967.

*Znamierowski, Nell. *Step-by-Step Weaving.* New York: Golden Press, 1967.

* Out of print but may be found in libraries and used bookstores.

Index